2ND Edition

BEST ⛺ TENT
Camping

OHIO

YOUR CAR-CAMPING GUIDE TO SCENIC BEAUTY, THE SOUNDS
OF NATURE, AND AN ESCAPE FROM CIVILIZATION

Best Tent Camping: Ohio

Copyright © 2012 and 2020 by Robert Loewendick
All rights reserved
Printed in China
Published by Menasha Ridge Press
Distributed by Publishers Group West
Second edition, first printing

Library of Congress Cataloging-in-Publication Data

Names: Loewendick, Robert, author.
Title: Best tent camping : Ohio : your car-camping guide to scenic beauty, the sounds of nature, and an escape
   from civilization / Robert Loewendick.
Description: Second edition. | Birmingham, AL : Menasha Ridge Press, [2020] | Series: Best tent camping
Identifiers: LCCN 2019051431 (print) | LCCN 2019051432 (ebook)
   ISBN 9781634042895 (paperback) | ISBN 9781634042901 (ebook)
Subjects: LCSH: Camping—Ohio—Guidebooks. | Camp sites, facilities, etc.—Ohio—Guidebooks. |
   Ohio—Guidebooks.
Classification: LCC GV191.42.O3 L64 2020 (print) | LCC GV191.42.O3 (ebook) | DDC 796.5109771—dc23
LC record available at https://lccn.loc.gov/2019051431
LC ebook record available at https://lccn.loc.gov/2019051432

Editor: Holly Cross
Cover and book design: Jonathan Norberg
Maps: Steve Jones and Robert Loewendick
Photos: Robert Loewendick, except as noted on page
Proofreader: Emily Beaumont
Indexer: Rich Carlson

MENASHA RIDGE PRESS
An imprint of AdventureKEEN
2204 First Ave. S., Ste. 102
Birmingham, AL 35233
800-443-7227, fax 205-326-1012

Visit menasharidge.com for a complete listing of our books and for ordering information. Contact us at our website, at
facebook.com/menasharidge, or at twitter.com/menasharidge with questions or comments. To find out more about
who we are and what we're doing, visit blog.menasharidge.com.

Cover: main photo: Hocking Hills State Park (see page 76); *inset photo:* Beaver Creek State Park (see page 25);
both photos by Robert Loewendick

2ND Edition

BEST TENT Camping

OHIO

YOUR CAR-CAMPING GUIDE TO SCENIC BEAUTY, THE SOUNDS OF NATURE, AND AN ESCAPE FROM CIVILIZATION

Robert Loewendick

 MENASHA RIDGE PRESS

Your Guide to the Outdoors Since 1982

Ohio Campground Locator Map

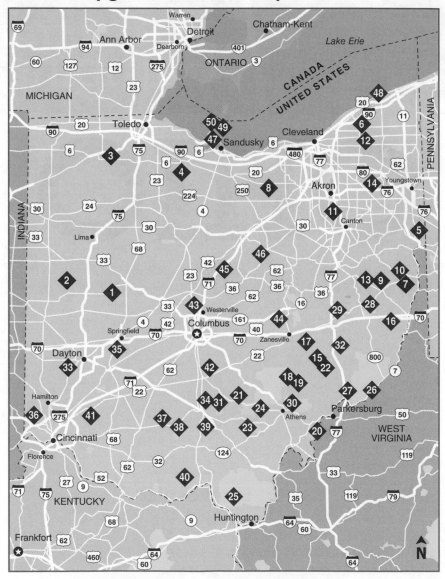

CONTENTS

SOUTHWEST 113

CENTRAL 141

LAKE ERIE REGION 158

Map Legend

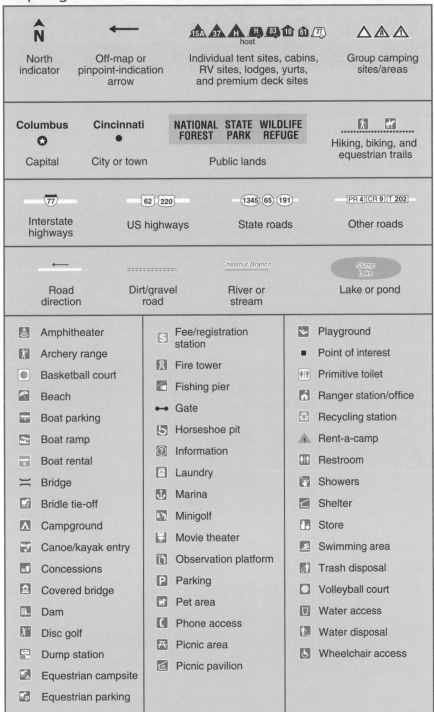

N — North indicator

← — Off-map or pinpoint-indication arrow

15A 37 H H. 83 10 61 27 — Individual tent sites, cabins, RV sites, lodges, yurts, and premium deck sites (host)

△ ⚠ ⚠ — Group camping sites/areas

Columbus ✪ — Capital

Cincinnati ● — City or town

NATIONAL FOREST STATE PARK WILDLIFE REFUGE — Public lands

Hiking, biking, and equestrian trails

77 — Interstate highways

62 220 — US highways

1345 65 191 — State roads

PR 4 CR 9 T 202 — Other roads

← — Road direction

Dirt/gravel road

Chestnut Branch — River or stream

Stump Lake — Lake or pond

Amphitheater	Fee/registration station	Playground
Archery range	Fire tower	Point of interest
Basketball court	Fishing pier	Primitive toilet
Beach	Gate	Ranger station/office
Boat parking	Horseshoe pit	Recycling station
Boat ramp	Information	Rent-a-camp
Boat rental	Laundry	Restroom
Bridge	Marina	Showers
Bridle tie-off	Minigolf	Shelter
Campground	Movie theater	Store
Canoe/kayak entry	Observation platform	Swimming area
Concessions	Parking	Trash disposal
Covered bridge	Pet area	Volleyball court
Dam	Phone access	Water access
Disc golf	Picnic area	Water disposal
Dump station	Picnic pavilion	Wheelchair access
Equestrian campsite		
Equestrian parking		

ACKNOWLEDGMENTS

Researching and writing this second edition of *Best Tent Camping: Ohio* was nearly as fun and challenging as creating the first edition. I must thank the following people for their willingness to share their time and talents by answering my calls and providing updated information. I tip my hat to the following.

My AdventureKEEN acquisitions editor, Tim Jackson, and his staff for the opportunity to research and write Ohio's tent-camping story and for presenting it to you in an entertaining and informative book.

Heidi Hetzel-Evans, communications manager of the Ohio Department of Natural Resources, and her intern, Libby Hosler, for answering my questions and providing elusive details of information when I requested them. Thanks to the dedicated state park employees who keep Ohio's parks in order, and to the friends of the parks organizations for their countless hours of donated time and talents.

Big thanks to the information officers of the metroparks, conservation districts, and national forests: Christina Boyer, Sandy Ward, Nathan Gerhart, Kimberly Whitton, Adria Bergeron, and Gary Chancey.

To my parents, for providing nearly endless access to the outdoors, with love and guidance, and to my four siblings who have all been my adventuring partners at one time or another.

To my wife, Linda, who is a fantastic traveling companion, whether it is a visit to an Ohio campground or across the country and beyond. And for sharing life's adventures hand in hand with me for 32 years.

To my daughter, Danielle, and son, Rob, great explorers in their own rights and my best, lifelong camping buddies.

—Robert Loewendick

PREFACE

Avid tent campers exploring the states east of the Mississippi River have dozens of ideal options. Ohio is definitely one of them. No, Ohio doesn't hold the mountains of Maine or Tennessee, or secluded forest camping like West Virginia or Vermont, but it does offer some of the best tent camping in the country, and in places that boast an abundance of natural resources. I traveled around and through the state in search of those places that may have an edge over others—and I found them.

For this second edition of Best Tent Camping Ohio, I reviewed and/or revisited the campgrounds that I included in the first edition, and I've added a few new ones. During the six months I worked on updating and adding to this second edition, I was reminded of just how enjoyable tent camping in my home state is. Ohio's diverse landscape is a treat to experience, from rivers and lakes to quiet woodlots with natural bounties and heavily forested gorges. It was a pleasure to pitch my tent in these places and absorb the serenity they presented. My experiences are revealed in the pages of this book, as are suggestions that will assist you in exploring Ohio by tent camping.

While visiting many of these campgrounds, I met the dedicated staff and volunteers who massage the parks with loving hands and hearts. Those folks also shared with me their opinions of what made their park unique and how to experience it for myself—and for you. Most of my stays were just one-nighters, but with the scoop from the locals, I knew what I must see and do. Some of the attractions were in the campground, or near it, while others were a short hike or paddle from camp, and some required a 5-mile drive or so. Wherever the adventure was, it was worth the trip.

Of the 50 campgrounds detailed in this book, 38 are owned and managed by the Ohio Department of Parks and Watercraft (ODPW). The ODPW is performing multiple campground improvements at various parks, now and during the next few years. Most upgrades are for RV enthusiasts, but tent campers will appreciate the new pit toilets and other amenities. As you visit campgrounds managed by the ODPW, expect a few pleasant surprises, as the improvements continue to be completed and may not be included in the descriptions in this book.

During my Ohio campground explorations, I made it a point to talk not only with management staff, but also with fellow tent campers. Those campers happily provided their opinions regarding what they enjoyed or disliked. I added their observations to my research cooking pot as an ingredient to create a profile of each campground with an accurate viewpoint. I have revealed the highlights of each destination, but there are also details that you will enjoy discovering on your own. And Ohio has much to discover, so pack the tent and camp box and get started!

BEST CAMPGROUNDS

BEST FOR BIRD-WATCHING

BEST FOR CANOEING AND KAYAKING

BEST FOR CYCLING AND MOUNTAIN BIKING

BEST FOR EQUESTRIANS

BEST FOR FAMILIES WITH KIDS

BEST FOR FISHING AND BOATING

BEST FOR FISHING AND BOATING *(continued)*

BEST FOR HIKING

BEST FOR PRIVACY AND SOLITUDE

BEST FOR SCENIC VISTAS AND PHOTOGRAPHY

BEST FOR SWIMMING

The sight and sounds of Lake Erie are a welcome way to start the morning at South Bass Island State Park (see page 168).

INTRODUCTION

A WORD ABOUT OHIO TENT CAMPING

Ohio's diversity of recreational opportunities is as varied as the state's geography. From fishing Lake Erie to hiking the Hocking Hills Region, from paddling the Little Miami River north of Cincinnati to touring wineries of the northeast, Ohio is a legitimate travel destination. Exploring Ohio's treasures while tent camping puts visitors one on one with a landscape and culture that appreciate life's simple pleasures.

The Muskingum Water Conservancy District manages several lakes in the east-central region that attract boaters and anglers. Salt Fork State Park, Ohio's largest, is a grand park for sure. Just about every outdoors activity you can think of happens there. The Wayne National Forest covers nearly half of the southeastern region. From auto tours that follow the Little Muskingum River, to paddling tranquil lakes that lie in the valleys of the rugged hills, this corner of Ohio presents an inviting tent-camping experience. Primitive camping enthusiasts will appreciate American Electric Power's Recreation Lands, which are reclaimed coal mining lands that host more than 350 ponds and four primitive campgrounds.

The hills meet the flatlands in the southwestern corner of the state. Slip into Shawnee State Forest, nicknamed The Little Smokies for good reason. Great Seal and Scioto Trail State Parks are in the heart of American Indian lands, and several parks present American Indian culture with burial mounds and museums.

Some of the most scenic camping in the state is on the Lake Erie Islands. South Bass Island puts campers on sites with vistas overlooking the great lake. Reachable by ferry, the islands are a summer vacation destination. If the island campgrounds are full, or mainland camping is your preference, East Harbor State Park campground provides an enjoyable tent-camping adventure.

For an adventurous blend of river, rugged hills, and primitive camping, the Mohican-Loudonville area between Cleveland and Columbus is the place. Clear Fork Gorge is a photographer's dream. Large hemlocks, rock outcrops, and waterfalls are the backdrop to this camping region.

The camping season in Ohio stretches from April to November at most campgrounds. Most Ohio State Parks are open year-round, but most shower houses and water supplies are turned off during winter; this depends on the individual park, so check the descriptions. If you're geared up correctly, spending a night in Ohio's winter landscape is refreshing. Winters can last a few months, so as soon as there is a hint of spring in the air, campers come out of their dens ready for some outdoor recreation. In spring, it's a good idea to make a reservation or have a plan B if you are using the first-come, first-serve method.

Summer camping vacations are a common practice in Ohio, so you will find a few popular campgrounds occupied in the middle of the week. Ohio summers feel like Florida during July and August because of the high humidity that blankets the state with temperatures in the 90s. Plan to pack a lot of ice to keep food safe and to create plenty of drinking water. Wooded sites are especially popular, with campers looking for a cool spot. When camping in the hill country, pick a site on a north-facing slope to drop the air temp at camp another few degrees.

October brings out the leaf peepers, especially across the southern half of the Buckeye State. Camping in Ohio during autumn is as good as tent camping gets. Enjoy the aroma of falling leaves mixed with the smell of a campfire floating about the campground, cool nights for sleeping and warm days for relaxing or adventuring, and sights that demand multiple photos of each brightly colored scene.

So toss this book in the car and begin your tour of Ohio's natural destinations.

HOW TO USE THIS GUIDEBOOK

THE RATINGS AND RATING CATEGORIES

As with all books in the Best Tent Camping series, this author personally experienced dozens of campgrounds and campsites to select the top 50 locations in this state. Within that universe of 50 sites, the author then ranked each one in the six categories described below. As a tough grader, the author awarded few five-star ratings, but each campground in this guidebook is superlative in its own way. For example, a site may be rated only one star in one category but perhaps five stars in another category. This rating system allows you to choose your destination based on the attributes that are most important to you.

★★★★★ The site is **ideal** in that category.

★★★★ The site is **exemplary** in that category.

★★★ The site is **very good** in that category.

★★ The site is **above average** in that category.

★ The site is **acceptable** in that category.

BEAUTY

Beauty, of course, is in the eye of the beholder, but panoramic views or proximity to a lake or river earn especially high marks. A campground that blends in well with the environment scores well, as do areas with remarkable wildlife or geology. Well-kept vegetation and nicely laid-out sites also up the ratings.

PRIVACY

The number of sites in a campground, the amount of screening between them, and physical distance from one another are decisive factors for the privacy ratings. Other considerations include the presence of nearby trails or day-use areas, and proximity to a town or city that would invite regular day-use traffic and perhaps compromise privacy.

SPACIOUSNESS

The size of the tent spot, its proximity to other tent spots, and whether or not it is defined or bordered from activity areas are the key considerations. The highest ratings go to sites that allow the tent camper to comfortably spread out without overlapping neighboring sites or picnic, cooking, or parking areas.

QUIET

Criteria for this rating include several touchstones: the author's experience at the site, the nearness of roads, the proximity of towns and cities, the probable number of RVs, the likelihood of noisy all-terrain vehicles or boats, and whether a campground host is available or willing to enforce the quiet hours. Of course, one set of noisy neighbors can deflate a five-star rating into a one-star (or no-star), so the latter criterion—campground enforcement—was particularly important in the author's evaluation in this category.

SECURITY

How you determine a campground's security will depend on who you view as the greater risk: other people or the wilderness. The more remote the campground, the less likely you are to run into opportunistic crime but the harder it is to get help in case of an accident or dangerous wildlife confrontation. Ratings in this category take into consideration whether there is a campground host or resident park ranger, proximity of other campers' sites, how much day traffic the campground receives, how close the campground is to a town or city, and whether there is cell phone reception or some type of phone or emergency call button.

CLEANLINESS

A campground's appearance often depends on who was there right before you and how your visit coincides with the maintenance schedule. In general, higher marks went to those campgrounds with hosts who cleaned up regularly. The rare case of odor-free toilets also gleaned high marks. At unhosted campgrounds, criteria included trash receptacles and evidence that sites were cleared and that signs and buildings were kept repaired. Markdowns for the campground were not given for a single visitor's garbage left at a site, but old trash in the shrubbery and along trails, indicating infrequent cleaning, did secure low ratings.

THE CAMPGROUND PROFILE

Each profile contains a concise but informative narrative that describes the campground and individual sites. Readers get a sense not only of the property itself but also of the recreational opportunities available nearby. This descriptive text is enhanced with three helpful sidebars: Ratings, Key Information, and Getting There (accurate driving directions that lead you to the campground from the nearest major roadway, along with GPS coordinates).

THE CAMPGROUND LOCATOR MAP AND MAP LEGEND

Use the campground locator map on page iv to pinpoint the location of each campground. The campground's number appears not only on the locator map but also in the table of contents and on the profile's first page. A map legend that details the symbols found on the campground-layout maps appears on page vii.

CAMPGROUND-LAYOUT MAPS

Each profile contains a detailed map of campground sites, internal roads, facilities, and other key items.

GPS CAMPGROUND-ENTRANCE COORDINATES

All of the profiles in this guidebook include the GPS coordinates for each site entrance. The intersection of the latitude (north) and longitude (west) coordinates orient you at the entrance. Please note that this guidebook uses the degree–decimal minute format for presenting the GPS coordinates. For example, the GPS coordinates for Kiser Lake State Park (page 12) are as follows:

N40° 10.979′ W83° 56.934′

To convert GPS coordinates from degrees, minutes, and seconds to the above degree–decimal minute format, the seconds are divided by 60. For more on GPS technology, visit usgs.gov.

WEATHER

Spring is the most variable season. During March, the hardwood trees begin to bud and the nights remain cool. Both winter- and summerlike weather can occur in spring. As summer approaches, the temperatures head for the 80s and often spike into the 90s. Summertime thunderstorms are brief but wild at times, with strong wind gusts. In fall, warm days and cool nights are the norm. The first snows of winter usually arrive in December, and snow falls intermittently through March. About 40–120 inches of snow can fall during this time. Expect to have entire days of below-freezing weather, though temperatures may range from mild to bitterly cold.

FLORA AND FAUNA PRECAUTIONS

SNAKES Ohio has a variety of snakes—including garter, black rat, and racers—most of which are benign. Timber rattlesnakes are occasionally spotted along the forested hills in extreme southern Ohio. Copperheads are more common across the southern half of the state and can be fairly aggressive if agitated.

When hiking, stick to well-used trails and wear over-the-ankle boots and loose-fitting long pants. Rattlesnakes like to bask in the sun and won't bite unless threatened. Do not step or put your hands where you cannot see, and avoid wandering around in the dark. Step on logs and rocks, never over them, and be especially careful when climbing rocks or gathering firewood.

TICKS Ticks are often found on brush and tall grass, waiting to hitch a ride on a warm-blooded passerby. They are most active during the summer months. You can use several strategies to reduce your chances of ticks getting under your skin. Some people choose to wear light-colored clothing, so ticks can be spotted

Photo by Jim Gathany/Centers for Disease Control and Prevention (public domain)

Deer tick

before they make it to the skin. Most important, be sure to visually check your hair, back of neck, armpits, and socks at the end of the hike. During your posthike shower, take a moment to do a more complete body check. For ticks that are already embedded, removal with tweezers is best. Use disinfectant solution on the wound.

POISON IVY Poison ivy is a common plant growing throughout Ohio. Recognizing and avoiding poison ivy is the most effective way to prevent the painful, itchy rashes associated with these plants. Poison ivy occurs as a vine or groundcover, three leaflets to a leaf. Urushiol, the oil in the sap of poison ivy, is responsible for the rash. Within 14 hours of exposure, raised lines and/or blisters will appear on the affected area, accom-

Photo by Tom Watson

panied by a terrible itch. Refrain from scratching because bacteria under your fingernails can cause an infection. Wash and dry the rash thoroughly, applying a calamine lotion to help dry out the rash. If itching or blistering is severe, seek medical attention. If you do come into contact with one of these plants, remember that oil-contaminated clothes, pets, or hiking gear can easily cause an irritating rash on you or someone else, so wash not only any exposed parts of your body but also clothes, gear, and pets if applicable.

FIRST AID KIT

A useful first aid kit may contain more items than you might think necessary. These are just the basics. Prepackaged kits in waterproof bags are available. As a preventive measure, take along sunscreen and insect repellent. Even though quite a few items are listed here, they pack down into a small space.

- Ace bandages or Spenco joint wraps
- Adhesive bandages
- Antibiotic ointment (such as Neosporin)
- Antihistamine (such as Benadryl), for mild allergies
- Antiseptic or disinfectant (such as Betadine or hydrogen peroxide)
- Aspirin, acetaminophen (Tylenol), or ibuprofen (Advil)
- Butterfly-closure bandages
- Comb and tweezers (for removing ticks from your skin)
- Emergency/survival blanket
- Epinephrine (EpiPen), for serious allergies
- Gauze (one roll and six 4-by-4-inch compress pads)
- LED flashlight or headlamp
- Matches or lighter

- Mirror (for signaling rescuers)
- Moist towelettes
- Moleskin/Spenco 2nd Skin
- Pocketknife or multipurpose tool
- Waterproof first aid tape
- Whistle (if you get lost or hurt)

HELPFUL HINTS FOR CAMPING IN OHIO

- **KNOW ABOUT PERMITS AND ACCESS.** All of Ohio's State Parks are accessible without a permit to visit. Some of the metro parks may charge a small entry fee, which is payable at the park entrance. The AEP Recreational Lands require a user permit to camp, fish, or simply explore. To get a free permit, visit AEP's website at aep.com/recreation/areas/recreationland, or by visiting one of the regional sporting goods stores and bait shops surrounding the recreational lands.

- **SMARTPHONES ARE HANDY NAVIGATIONAL DEVICES,** but an updated, printed road map is a nice companion to have along, as several roads have been abandoned and you may end up at a dead end. Ohio's gravel county and township roads are like driving on marbles during the summer road-grading season. Slow down and enjoy the view, and not from ditch.

- **CONSIDER STORMS.** The northern edge of Ohio is Lake Erie's shoreline. Storms come off the lake quickly and intensely throughout the spring and summer, so keep an eye on the horizon. Summer afternoon storms also form quickly and often release heavy downpours. When camping in the deep valleys of southern Ohio, consider this before leaving for your camping trip. During the last decade, several Ohio campgrounds that lie at the bottom of sharp valleys have dealt with flash flooding.

- **DISPERSED CAMPING IS AN OPTION.** The Wayne National Forest is split into three sections across southeastern Ohio. Although several destinations within the forest offer designated campsites, dispersed camping is also allowed. Camping is permitted on national forest lands anywhere that camping equipment or a vehicle does not block developed trails or right-of-ways. There is no charge for dispersed camping in the Wayne, but you must carry out any trash and abide the 14-day minimum stay law.

- **EXPLORE NATURAL AREAS.** The Ohio Department of Natural Resources Department of Natural Areas and Preserves (DNAP) maintains 136 sites across the state. The natural areas are pristine places for visitors to observe (don't touch!) Ohio's true flora and fauna. Contact the DNAP for more information at 614-265-6561.

TIPS FOR A HAPPY CAMPING TRIP

There is nothing worse than a bad camping trip, especially because it is so easy to have a great time. To assist with making your outing a happy one, here are some pointers.

- **RESERVE YOUR SITE AHEAD OF TIME.** During the summer season and fall foliage season, it's best to reserve a campsite if possible. Camping in Ohio during these seasons is popular, and securing a campsite can be a challenge. For first-come, first-serve sites, call ahead to the campground office to find out if those sites are still available. Without calling ahead, showing up on Friday as early as possible will increase your odds of grabbing a site.

- **PICK YOUR CAMPING BUDDIES WISELY.** A family trip is pretty straightforward, but you may want to reconsider including grumpy Uncle Fred, who doesn't like bugs, sunshine, or marshmallows. After you know who's going, make sure that everyone is on the same page regarding expectations of difficulty (amenities or the lack thereof, physical exertion, and so on), sleeping arrangements, and food requirements.

- **DON'T DUPLICATE EQUIPMENT** such as cooking pots and lanterns among campers in your party. Carry what you need to have a good time, but don't turn the trip into a major moving experience.

- **DRESS FOR THE SEASON.** Be informed on the temperature highs and lows of the specific area you plan to visit. It may be warm at night in the summer in your backyard, but up in the hills or hollows it is a bit more chilly. Bring extra clothes, wear layers, and plan for extremes.

- **PITCH YOUR TENT ON A LEVEL SURFACE,** preferably one covered with leaves, pine straw, or grass. Use a tarp or specially designed footprint to thwart ground moisture and to protect the tent floor. Do a little site maintenance, such as picking up the small rocks and sticks that can damage your tent floor and make sleep uncomfortable. If you have a separate tent rain fly but don't think you'll need it, keep it rolled up at the base of the tent in case it starts raining at midnight.

- **TAKE A SLEEPING PAD** if you don't like sleeping on the ground. Get one that is full-length and thicker than you think you might need. This will not only keep your hips from aching on hard ground, but it will also help keep you warm. A wide range of thin, light, inflatable pads is available at camping stores today, and these are a much better choice than home air mattresses, which conduct heat away from the body and tend to deflate during the night.

- **PLAN TASTY, FUN, AND EASY MEALS.** If you're not backpacking, there is no need to skimp on food due to weight, so bring everything you will need to prepare, cook, eat, and clean up.

- **IF YOU TEND TO USE THE BATHROOM AT NIGHT, PLAN ACCORDINGLY.** Keep a flashlight, shoes, and whatever else you might need by the tent door, and know exactly where to head in the dark.

- **STANDING DEAD TREES AND STORM-DAMAGED LIVING TREES CAN POSE A REAL HAZARD** to tent campers. These trees may have loose or broken limbs that could fall at any time. When choosing a campsite or even just a spot to rest during a hike, look up.

CAMPING ETIQUETTE

Camping experiences can vary wildly depending on a variety of factors, such as weather, preparedness, fellow campers, and time of year. Here are a few tips on how to create good vibes with fellow campers and wildlife you encounter.

- **OBTAIN ALL PERMITS AND AUTHORIZATION AS REQUIRED.** Make sure you check in, pay your fee, and mark your site as directed. Don't make the mistake of grabbing a seemingly empty site that looks more appealing than your site. It could be reserved. If you're unhappy with the site you've selected, check with the campground host for other options.

- **LEAVE ONLY FOOTPRINTS.** Be sensitive to the ground beneath you. Be sure to place all garbage in designated receptacles or pack it out if none are available. No one likes to see the trash someone else has left behind.

- **NEVER SPOOK ANIMALS.** It's common for animals to wander through campsites, where they may be accustomed to the presence of humans (and our food). An unannounced approach, a sudden movement, or a loud noise startles most animals. A surprised animal can be dangerous to you, to others, and to themselves. Give them plenty of space.

- **PLAN AHEAD.** Know your equipment, your ability, and the area where you are camping—and prepare accordingly. Be self-sufficient at all times; carry necessary supplies for changes in weather or other conditions. A well-executed trip is a satisfaction to you and to others.

- **BE COURTEOUS TO OTHER CAMPERS,** hikers, bikers, and others you encounter. This stuff is common sense, but like a lot of common sense, it bears repeating. Be aware of quiet hours, especially when pulling into a campground after dark. Avoid shining your headlights or flashlights into other campsites as you are searching for a spot. And please turn down your car stereo; that bass beat carries far in the night air. Always walk on designated paths and roads, and respect the privacy of your neighbors by not strolling through their site to get to the restrooms. You'll also reduce damage to the foliage and keep the campground green by sticking to the main trail. Please clean up after yourself. Make cleaning up into a game with your kids: whoever packs out the most candy papers, pop cans, and gum wrappers is the winner.

- **STRICTLY FOLLOW THE CAMPGROUND'S RULES** regarding the building of fires. Never burn trash. Trash smoke smells horrible, and trash debris in a fire pit or grill is unsightly.

A WORD ABOUT BACKCOUNTRY CAMPING

Following these guidelines will increase your chances for a pleasant, safe, and low-impact interaction with nature.

- **ADHERE TO THE ADAGES "PACK IT IN, PACK IT OUT" AND "TAKE ONLY PICTURES, LEAVE ONLY FOOTPRINTS."** A permit is not required before entering the backcountry to camp in the Wayne National Forest. However, you should practice Leave No Trace camping ethics while in the backcountry.

- **IN OHIO, OPEN FIRES ARE PERMITTED** except during dry times when the forest service may issue a fire ban. Backpacking stoves are strongly encouraged.

- **BURY SOLID HUMAN WASTE** in a hole at least 3 inches deep and at least 200 feet away from trails and water sources; a trowel is basic backpacking equipment. More often, however, the practice of burying human waste is being banned. Using a portable waste bag (which come in various forms but are basically glorified plastic bags) may seem unthinkable at first, but it's really no big deal. Just bring an extra large zip-top bag for extra insurance against structural failures.

VENTURING AWAY FROM THE CAMPGROUND

If you go for a hike, bike, or other excursion into the wilderness, here are some tips:

- **ALWAYS CARRY FOOD AND WATER,** whether you are planning to go overnight or not. Food will give you energy, help keep you warm, and sustain you

Sun filters through the trees on a misty morning at Lake Loramie State Park (see page 15).

Photo courtesy of Ohio Department of Natural Resources

in an emergency until help arrives. Bring potable water or treat water by boiling or filtering before drinking from a lake or stream.

- **STAY ON DESIGNATED TRAILS.** Most hikers get lost when they leave the trail. Even on the most clearly marked trails, there is usually a point where you have to stop and consider which direction to head. If you become disoriented, don't panic. As soon as you think you may be off-track, stop, assess your current direction, and then retrace your steps back to the point where you went awry. If you have absolutely no idea how to continue, return to the trailhead the way you came in. Should you become completely lost and have no idea of how to return to the trailhead, remaining in place along the trail and waiting for help is most often the best option for adults and always the best option for children.

- **BE ESPECIALLY CAREFUL WHEN CROSSING STREAMS.** Whether you are fording the stream or crossing on a log, make every step count. If you have any doubt about maintaining your balance on a log, go ahead and ford the stream instead. When fording a stream, use a trekking pole or stout stick for balance and face upstream as you cross. If a stream seems too deep to ford, turn back. Whatever is on the other side is not worth risking your life.

- **BE CAREFUL AT OVERLOOKS.** Although these areas may provide spectacular views, they are potentially hazardous. Stay back from the edge of outcrops and be absolutely sure of your footing: a misstep can mean a nasty and possibly fatal fall.

- **KNOW THE SYMPTOMS OF HYPOTHERMIA.** Shivering and forgetfulness are the two most common indicators of this insidious killer. Hypothermia can occur at any elevation, even in the summer. Wearing cotton clothing puts you especially at risk because cotton, when wet, wicks heat away from the body. To prevent hypothermia, dress in layers using synthetic clothing for insulation; use a cap and gloves to reduce heat loss; and protect yourself with waterproof, breathable outerwear. If symptoms arise, take the victim to shelter, start a fire if you can, give hot liquids, and put the person in dry clothes or a dry sleeping bag.

- **TAKE ALONG YOUR BRAIN.** A cool, calculating mind is the single most important piece of equipment you'll ever need on the trail. Think before you act. Watch your step. Plan ahead. Avoiding accidents before they happen is the best recipe for a rewarding and relaxing hike.

NORTHWEST

Forests and lakes are rare treats of Ohio's flat Northwest landscape
(see Kiser Lake State park, page 12).

⛺Kiser Lake State Park

Beauty ★★★ Privacy ★★ Spaciousness ★★ Quiet ★★★ Security ★★★ Cleanliness ★★★

The glaciers shaped Kiser's diverse landscape of wetlands, forest, and lake.

This quiet, smaller park (531 acres) offers big benefits to campers wanting to get away. Surrounded by wooded hills and diverse wetlands, Kiser State Park is a wildlife viewers' gold mine. This varied landscape was created by glaciers that left deposits of boulders, sand, and gravel. Much of the sand and many of the boulders were gathered by the glaciers as they headed south from Canada. The rocks found lying around the short hills and washes surrounding the lake today are those same rocks from the glacial period.

This area was also the home of Tecumseh, the great Shawnee warrior. Hiking the 11 miles of park trails reveals the natural amenities that supported the American Indians of the area. For anglers, five stone fishing piers are placed around the lake near various forms of game fish habitat. Kiser Lake is off limits to boats with engines, so feel free to paddle away without any wakes to contend with while trying to get that close-up water photo.

A diverse campground starts at the lake's southern shoreline and extends up into the woods. Arriving from the south, the campground entrance is on the right after passing a stately row of weeping willows. The lake is on the left, and along its shore are 14 sites sprinkled about the 50-yard distance from the road to the lake. In the main section of the campground you will find sites 30–51 in orderly rows in full sun. Slide through that group and find tent-only site 29 as the campground lane curves along the southern edge and heads toward a wood grove. Sites 23–28 are on the right as you approach the wood grove, and although they're a bit small and close to the park road, all are comfortable and have a woodland backing.

Hikers can explore Kiser Lake's surrounding forest on the Red Oak Trail.

KEY INFORMATION

LOCATION: 4370 Kiser Lake Road
St. Paris, Ohio 43072

CONTACT: 937-362-3565,
parks.ohiodnr.gov/kiserlake

OPEN: Year-round; limited facilities in winter

SITES: 56 nonelectric, 20 electric

EACH SITE HAS: Picnic table, fire ring

WHEELCHAIR ACCESS: Sites 39 and 40 are
ADA-accessible.

ASSIGNMENT: Walk-in sites first come,
first served; others may be reserved at
866-644-6727 or ohiostateparks.reserve
america.com

REGISTRATION: Self-registration station at
campground entrance

AMENITIES: Pit toilets, camp store, boat
rental, sports courts, playground, swimming
beach, nature center

PARKING: At each site

FEE: $22 nonelectric, $26 electric;
deduct $3 in winter

ELEVATION: 1,108 feet

RESTRICTIONS

PETS: On leash only

QUIET HOURS: 10 p.m.–7 a.m.

FIRES: In fire ring, which must not be moved

ALCOHOL: Prohibited in public areas in every
state park but may be consumed within the
confines of a rented cabin, cabin site, lodge
room, or campsite

VEHICLES: 2/site

OTHER: Gathering firewood prohibited;
maximum 6 people/site

Sites 12–22 line both sides of the 200-foot paved lane leading through the center of the wood grove. Sites 21 and 22 are tent-only sites and are reservable, not walk-in sites. The Ohio State Parks system titles non-reservable sites as walk-in sites. The term *walk-in* may mislead campers to think that a walk-in site requires a short trek to reach the site. However, a walk-in site at Ohio State Parks means the site is available for anyone walking in to the campground in need of a site. At the cul-de-sac at the head of the wood grove are sites 15 and 16, which are great tent sites because they're enveloped in the trees and require a short walk (10 yards) to reach them. The Red Oak Trail passes by site 18 and connects with the Boardwalk trail to the west.

The Boardwalk trail guides visitors through the Kiser Lake Wetlands—a 51-acre state nature preserve. The Boardwalk is also accessible from a small parking area 0.2 mile south of the campground entrance. The wetlands include two prairie fens that are home to numerous rare plant species, animals, and insects. The giant swallowtail butterfly and the northern ravine salamander are two residents you may see while walking along the 0.6-mile, looping Boardwalk.

Across the road from the main campground are those waterfront sites. Directly across from the main campground entrance are sites 66–71 spread around a small, paved circle; sites 67–70 are tent-only. Site 71 is the closest to the water, but it is also heavily visited by Canada geese, which leave behind unpleasant droppings that you must avoid stepping on or pitching a tent over. Sites 72–75 are across a drainage ditch to the north and accessible from their own paved road. Each of these sites has a shade tree and a wide view of the lake. Just to the north are sites 76–79, also separated by the same drainage ditch. Site 79, the only one with shade in this group, sits on the water's edge. During midsummer, expect mats of lily pads parked along the shoreline, which can make it tough to fish from the campsite.

Kiser Lake State Park

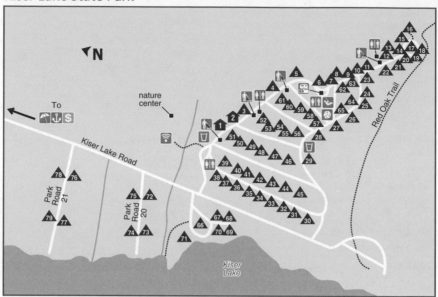

GETTING THERE

From Piqua, at Exit 82 on I-75, travel east on US 36 for 12.3 miles to OH 235 and turn left. Follow OH 235 north 3 miles to Possum Hollow Road and turn right. Go 1.5 miles to Kiser Lake Road, turn left, and follow it 0.8 mile to the campground entrance on the right.

GPS COORDINATES: N40° 10.979' W83° 56.934'

2

⛺ Lake Loramie State Park

Beauty ★★ Privacy ★★ Spaciousness ★★★ Quiet ★★★ Security ★★★★ Cleanliness ★★★★

Built in 1824, Lake Loramie fed the Miami and Erie Canal system, which is followed by hiking trails today.

Lake Loramie State Park is built around the remnants of the Miami and Erie Canal. The lake was constructed in 1824 to store water to supply the canal system that provided transportation between Lake Erie and the Ohio River. A section of the park's trail system follows the Miami and Erie Canal, which is also a part of the Buckeye Trail and the North Country National Scenic Trail. Plenty of historical sites are near, as are artisans displaying their skills during the spring, summer, and fall at a local art center neighboring the park.

In the campground, an assembly of bald cypress and sweet gum trees dates back to the 1950s. Fishing from the shore is easy at Lake Loramie, so don't forget your fishing gear. Picnic tables are liberally dispersed around the many lagoons on the west side of the lake, so a picnic is in order as well.

The flat lands of west central Ohio aren't among the state's regions targeted by many tent campers, but Lake Loramie State Park is an exception. The majority of the campground is frequented by RVers and may seem like a busy neighborhood during the summer vacation season. But the nonelectric sites that sit alone on a square peninsula, somewhat separated

Paddle Lake Loramie's 913 acres of no-wake water.   *Photo courtesy of Ohio Department of Natural Resources*

KEY INFORMATION

LOCATION: 4401 Ft. LoramieSwanders Road Minster, Ohio 45865

CONTACT: 937-295-2011, parks.ohiodnr.gov/lakeloramie

OPEN: Year-round; limited facilities in winter; water at dump station only

SITES: 15 nonelectric, 142 electric

EACH SITE HAS: Picnic table, fire ring

WHEELCHAIR ACCESS: Full-service sites 147 and 148, shower house, and restroom are all ADA-accessible.

ASSIGNMENT: Walk-in sites first come, first served; others may be reserved at 866-644-6727 or ohiostateparks.reserveamerica.com

REGISTRATION: Self-registration station at campground office, if campground office closed

AMENITIES: Showers, flush toilets, laundry, camp store, sports courts, playground, swimming beach, miniature golf, nature center, disc-golf course, fitness trail, kayak rentals, free Wi-Fi at camp office

PARKING: At each site

FEE: $22 nonelectric, $28 electric; deduct $3 in winter

ELEVATION: 950 feet

RESTRICTIONS

PETS: On leash only

QUIET HOURS: 10 p.m.–7 a.m.

FIRES: In fire ring, which must not be moved

ALCOHOL: Prohibited in public areas in every state park but may be consumed within the confines of a rented cabin, cabin site, lodge room, or campsite

VEHICLES: 2/site

OTHER: Gathering firewood prohibited; maximum 6 people/site

from the RV village, are an exception. Two sets of sites share the numbers 1–14. The first 14-site section is electric and is located a couple yards north of the campground office at the campground entrance. Ignore those sites. Instead, take a right after passing the campground office by site 135 on the right. Then take a left before site 152 and then an immediate right and cruise by sites 92–95. Next to site 95 is signage on the left directing you to the overflow parking access road; follow that. The peninsula, approximately 50 yards by 50 yards, is on the right. Dressed with a few massive oak trees standing in the middle are the nonelectric sites 1–14. Those are the ones you want, but be aware that they are not reservable.

The nonelectric section is not completely cut off from the two main camping areas, and the RVs are not completely out of sight, but the focus of the nonelectric sites is the lake channel that surrounds the peninsula. The channel, or canal, of Lake Loramie is nearly at ground level, so sliding a kayak into the water from the campsites is doable. Paddle the channel under the footbridge and out into bigger water if you dare. The nonelectric sites are split into two sections, but it's hard to tell because they appear to be one group.

As you arrive on the peninsula, you'll first encounter sites 1–4. There is only a hint of a path for your vehicle to follow to the sites from the gravel lane, but it's legal to drive on the grass at that point. These first four sites are at the water's edge, as are sites 5 and 6. Sites 7–9 are on the interior of the peninsula, completing a horseshoe shape that is one of the two sections. The second subsection of the peninsula has sites 10–14, which sit at the water's edge along the eastern shore of peninsula. Parking for those five sites is on the gravel loop that starts behind site 9 and ends at the front of site 14. These five sites are the picks of the litter because they face the canal laced with American lotus and the opposing bank that is covered with vegetation, which supports migrating waterfowl for viewing fun. A shower house and water supply are back by site 152.

The footbridge crossing the lake channel near site 14 leads to the 2-mile Lakeview Trail. This is an easy walk, and all level except for the bridge crossing. At the trail's turning point, at the Blackberry Island Access parking area, is another footbridge leading to the island. A nature trail follows the perimeter of the forested island and puts you one on one with the busy birdlife of the island.

Lake Loramie State Park

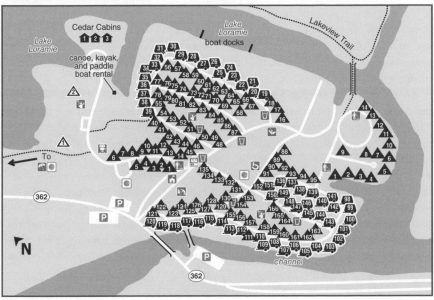

GETTING THERE

From I-75, take Exit 99 near Anna and go west on OH 119 for 11 miles to Minster. Turn left on South Paris Street at the outskirts of town, follow it to OH 362, and turn left. Follow OH 362 for 2.5 miles to the campground entrance on the left.

GPS COORDINATES: N40° 21.459' W84° 21.430'

3

⛺ Mary Jane Thurston State Park

Beauty ★★★ Privacy ★★ Spaciousness ★★★ Quiet ★★ Security ★★ Cleanliness ★★

Explore the historic Maumee River while camping beside it.

The Maumee River, a State Scenic River, has been a vital passageway for centuries and then some. American Indians utilized the river for sustenance and travel, and today, those two elements are still experienced there but on a recreational level. Mary Jane Thurston State Park provides access to the river and its supporting environment, especially on the southern riverbank west of Grand Rapids—a neat little river town that caters to visitors with stores, ice-cream shops, a great view of the river, and a historic canal system.

A day-use area and campground lie just west of Grand Rapids. The day-use area includes a small lodge overlooking the river and an observation deck. Keep your eye to the sky, as bald eagles are regularly spotted searching for a meal. Across the river, and about 5 miles upriver of the campground and day-use area, is the North Turkeyfoot area of the state park. To get there, leave the campground entrance and travel 7.4 miles west on OH 65 to a bridge; after crossing the bridge, turn right. On the right, you can explore the heavy river woodlands habitat on various hiking trails. Dispersed tent camping is allowed throughout North Turkeyfoot, but no fires are allowed.

Back at the campground, sit along the river's edge and ponder what it must have been like here a century ago, a lovely way to pass the time. Camping along this stretch of river continues

The Maumee River provides a beautiful backdrop for camping at Mary Jane Thurston State Park.

KEY INFORMATION

LOCATION: 1466 OH 65; McClure, Ohio 43534

CONTACT: 419-832-7662,
parks.ohiodnr.gov/maryjanethurston

OPEN: Year-round, but no water

SITES: 16 nonelectric, tent only; 23 electric

EACH SITE HAS: Picnic table, fire ring

WHEELCHAIR ACCESS: No specific
ADA-accessible sites

ASSIGNMENT: Walk-in sites first come, first
served; others may be reserved at 866-644-
6727 or ohiostateparks.reserveamerica.com

REGISTRATION: Self-registration station at
campground entrance

AMENITIES: Flush toilets, pit toilets, boat
launch

PARKING: At each site; in parking area for
tent-only sites

FEE: $22 nonelectric, $26 electric;
deduct $3 in winter

ELEVATION: 639 feet

RESTRICTIONS

PETS: On leash only

QUIET HOURS: 10 p.m.–7 a.m.

FIRES: In fire ring, which must not be moved

ALCOHOL: Prohibited in public areas in every
state park but may be consumed within the
confines of a rented cabin, cabin site, lodge
room, or campsite

VEHICLES: 2/site; no vehicles allowed
in tent area; tent campers use designated
parking area adjacent to tent area

OTHER: Gathering firewood prohibited;
maximum 6 people/site

the tradition of being close with the impressive, natural force. The campground consists of 39 sites, separated into two sections. Near the campground entrance are the first 14 sites, which are considered RV sites. Sites 1–4 are equipped with water hookups and electric. Site 2 is occupied by the campground host, who sells firewood through late spring, summer, and early fall camping seasons. At the back of site 2 is a footbridge that leads to the day-use area of the park. Sites 5–14 are on the left side of the campground road, opposite the first four. The sites are staged along both sides of a spur road that leads to a small parking area and the base of the sled hill. These sites are spacious and offer plenty of room for a boat trailer and a tent to fit comfortably.

Follow the gravel lane from the RV area through a woodlot and toward the Maumee River. As the river comes into view, sites 15 and 16 will be on the right, next to the playground. These sites fill a corner created by the river and a feeder creek to the east. Because these spots are the first to greet visitors, they experience several drive-bys during the day by sightseers. The same goes for sites 17–23, on around the corner and parallel to the river. Sites 24–39 are strung out in two equal rows running along the river and only a few feet above the water. During early spring rains, the campground may be closed due to flooding, so call ahead to confirm that the campground is dry. During times of normal river levels, the short, shallow falls within sight of the campground are commonly waded and explored as the bedrock is exposed. Site 24 is closest to the river from the parking lot. Site 39 is across the flat, grassy campground lawn, with a forested marsh at its backside. Site 32 is the farthest from the parking area, requiring a walk of 40 yards to reach it. Site 31 offers a wide, unobstructed view of the river and the falls. A hundred yards downstream are two dams—one on each side of a small island. The dams slow and deepen the water at that point, making it a turning point for boaters and water skiers, which are entertaining to watch while enjoying a riverside lunch at the campsite.

Site 30's river view is blocked by a short row of young trees, so if you're looking for a privacy screen from the river, this is the site for you. Site 25 blends with the river's edge for easy access to fishing or cooling your toes in the water working its way to Lake Erie, only 25 miles away. The Maumee River becomes crowded with walleye anglers during the spring spawning runs that begin when the water temps reach just above freezing. The main attraction is the river, so take advantage of the numerous ways to interact with it—whatever the season.

Mary Jane Thurston State Park

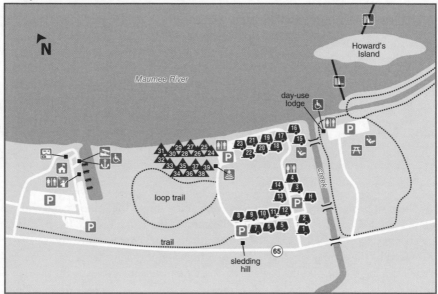

GETTING THERE

From I-75, take Exit 179 at Bowling Green and follow US 6 west 12.8 miles. Turn right on County Road 189 (Wapakoneta Road) and travel north 2.8 miles to OH 65 (W. Second St.). Turn left and go 0.7 mile to the campground entrance on the right.

GPS COORDINATES: N41° 24.575' W83° 52.658'

4

⛺ Wolf Creek Park

Beauty ★★ Privacy ★★★ Spaciousness ★★★ Quiet ★★★★ Security ★★ Cleanliness ★★★

This quiet campground lies on the bank of a State Scenic River.

The park got its name from the creek north of the park that is a tributary to the Sandusky River, a State Scenic River. The river received its scenic status in the early 1970s, the second river in the state to be tagged as such. The diverse 130-mile-long Sandusky River flows over stone falls at some points and then slowly courses along stretches of deeper pools and runs. Time flies while paddling the river and taking in picturesque views of the riverscapes. A day on the river also brings about an appetite for tasty camp cooking and an outing iced with a night under the open, northern Ohio sky. Wolf Creek Park provides just the right situation for that adventure.

Two nature trails explore the river environment at the water's edge and also away from the water through fields of wildflowers during spring and summer. Walking along the river's edge may bring back days of your youth, when creeks and rivers were the PlayStation of the times. On hot days, slip on some old tennis shoes, grab a small net, and wade in to see what you can find.

Although the campground runs along the western bank of the Sandusky River, the sites are not at the water's edge. Access to the river from even the closest campsite requires a

Quiet Wolf Creek Park features roomy campsites.

LOCATION: 2701 S. OH 53
Fremont, Ohio 43420

CONTACT: Operated by Sandusky
County Park District: 419-334-4495,
lovemyparks.com/parks/wolf_creek_park

OPEN: April 15–November 15

SITES: 24 primitive

EACH SITE HAS: Picnic table, fire ring

WHEELCHAIR ACCESS: None

ASSIGNMENT: Reservations required and
must be made online at lovemyparks.com

REGISTRATION: Register online at
lovemyparks.com

AMENITIES: Pit toilets, canoe launch ramp

PARKING: At each site

FEE: $15

ELEVATION: 667 feet

RESTRICTIONS

PETS: Must be leashed; never tether to a tree

QUIET HOURS: 11 a.m.–7 a.m.

FIRES: In fire ring

ALCOHOL: Prohibited

VEHICLES: 2/site

OTHER: Gathering firewood prohibited;
camp in designated areas only

20-yard walk through knee-high vegetation and trees growing on a steep bank. But once at the water, the view and river itself are a pleasant reward. On quiet nights you can still hear the water even with the tree and brush buffer between your site and the river. The first eight sites begin at the kiosk and border both sides of the gravel campground road. These are the smallest of the 24 sites. You may meet a backpacker or two while there, as the Buckeye Trail passes through the park.

The campground road passes through a pinch point with a wooded wash on both sides of the road. During times of high water, this wash may get wet, but there's no need to worry, as the elevation between the campground and the wash is over 20 feet. The next three sites

Sign in and relax with no crowds at Wolf Creek Park.

between the road and the river are the closest to the waterway. Each site has a footpath leading to the river, so you can make a quick cast or two with the fly rod before that simmering meal in the Dutch oven is ready to eat. Sites 16, 17, and 18 are on the river side as the campground road enters a 50-yard circle, where the remainder of the sites sit around the outer edge of the big loop surrounding a mowed lawn—perfect for chasing balls or flying a kite.

The summer weekend I visited the park, I was in one of only two occupied sites. The campground is quiet except for the traffic along OH 53, which can be busy during the day. The sites are well spread out with at least a dozen or so yards between them. Site 21 has a nature trail pass through it and onto the picnic area to the north of the campground and south back to the kiosk where it connects to another nameless nature trail.

From the campground entrance off OH 53, travel north 0.9 mile up the highway to the picnic area and canoe launch access road. The canoe launch ramp is all the way down a lane at the end of a large, gravel parking lot. Canoes and kayaks must be carried 75 feet down a paved decline to the river's edge. Down from the ramp is a small island splitting the river. For a 2-mile float down the Sandusky River, put in at the County Road 201 bridge north of the park and take out at the park's canoe launch ramp or at the gravel bank at the campground. The river is the reason for visiting this park. No matter what level of interaction you prefer with the pretty river, it's worth the time.

Wolf Creek Park

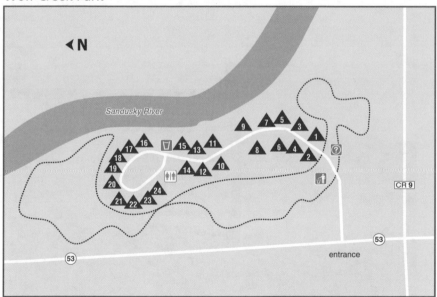

GETTING THERE

From Fremont, follow OH 53 south 5.5 miles to the campground entrance on the left.

GPS COORDINATES: N41° 15.839' W83° 10.100'

NORTHEAST

Be sure to visit the swimming beach at Tappan Lake (see page 49).

5

⛺ Beaver Creek State Park

Beauty ★★★★ Privacy ★★★ Spaciousness ★★★ Quiet ★★★ Security ★★★ Cleanliness ★★★

Explore the home of the Little Beaver Creek State and National Wild and Scenic River.

Coming from the north, it's soon apparent to visitors that they have arrived on the door-step of the Appalachian Mountains. Beaver Creek State Park covers 2,722 land acres and only 4 miles of river, but the river is the main attraction. Little Beaver Creek has been designated a National Wild and Scenic River and rightly so. Slip a kayak into its clear waters and shoot over a few, short rapids for some whitewater fun, or simply lean back and admire the cliffs that contain the river. At the center of the park is a pioneer village that relied on the river to turn millstones during the early 1800s. An iron bridge crosses the river at the village, which is also where the park office is. South of the village, 0.87 mile on Echo Dell Road, is the park's Wildlife Education Center, which features live animals and 300 mounted specimens. The center is open May–October on the weekends, 1–5 p.m.

Beaver Creek's family campground offers the picture-perfect place to pitch a tent. As soon as you pull into the campground, your mind will instantly transition to relax mode. Site 42 is the first one on the left; it's only a dozen yards beyond the entrance, but its appearance and layout resemble a campsite in a western forest, with big pines spaced far enough apart to make it feel open and a plush carpet of pine needles underfoot. After passing site 42, a road to the left leads to the best sites of the campground—sites 43–55. All are reservable.

Beaver Creek's beauty has attracted tent campers for centuries.

KEY INFORMATION

LOCATION: 12021 Echo Dell Road
East Liverpool, Ohio 43920

CONTACT: 330-385-3091,
parks.ohiodnr.gov/beavercreek

OPEN: Year-round; limited facilities in winter

SITES: 44 nonelectric, 6 electric

EACH SITE HAS: Picnic table, fire ring

WHEELCHAIR ACCESS: None

ASSIGNMENT: Walk-in sites first come,
first served; others may be reserved at
866-644-6727 or ohiostateparks.reserve
america.com

REGISTRATION: Self-registration station

AMENITIES: Pit toilets, sun shower, playground,
nature center, pioneer village, horseshoe pits,
archery range

PARKING: At each site

FEE: $24; deduct $1 from fee Sunday–
Thursday; deduct $3 in winter

ELEVATION: 1,102 feet

RESTRICTIONS

PETS: On leash only

QUIET HOURS: 10 p.m.–7 a.m.

FIRES: In fire ring, which must not be moved

ALCOHOL: Prohibited in public areas in every
state park but may be consumed within the
confines of a rented cabin, cabin site, lodge
room, or campsite

VEHICLES: 2/site

OTHER: Gathering firewood prohibited;
maximum 6 people/site

This shorter road of the campground has sites on the upper side only. Site 44 is several feet wider and deeper than the others, with white pines towering like giant soldiers. Site 46 lies in a slight swale that dips through the pine-covered ridge. Avoid this site if rain is in the forecast. This specific campground road goes 0.1 mile before ending at a cul-de-sac. Near the turnaround, site 50 invites tent campers to spread out on its wide layout. At the rear of these sites, the forest closes in and songbirds entertain while flittering about the open and dense woodland. There is a pit toilet across from site 48, but no water source is available in this section. Across from site 46 is the trailhead for the Dogwood Trail, which leads trekkers down to the star of this state park, Little Beaver Creek.

Back to the main campground road and near site 2 is a pit toilet and self-registration station with details posted regarding the park, campground, and any planned activities. Across the road from the registration station are the sun shower and the amphitheater. Sites 32 and 33 are situated farther off the road's edge than their neighboring sites. Next to the parking spaces for these two sites is a playground. It's the perfect scenario for a couple of tent-camping families with small children. Site 23 sits at the end of this second campground road and offers campers an overlook of the valley cut by the Little Beaver Creek centuries ago.

The North Country Trail (NCT), a 4,600-mile hiking trail that stretches from North Dakota to New York, meanders through Beaver Creek State Park for 6.3 miles. The NCT includes various hiking challenges, from creek crossings to roadside walks. Hiking at Beaver Creek is not to be hurried; don't simply walk through, but pause and absorb the diverse sights and sounds. Look for remnants of historic river locks while maneuvering along the trail near the river. Before hikers reach the valley floor and Little Beaver Creek, the trail winds around the sides of forested ridges that warrant enough pauses to enjoy the place. Hikers should allow an extra hour or two for the daily hike plan.

Beaver Creek State Park

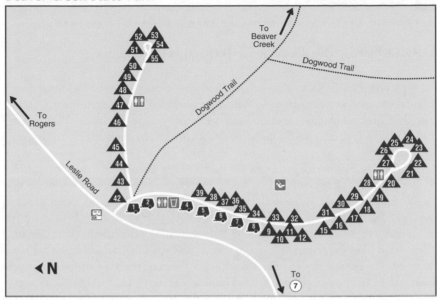

GETTING THERE

From East Liverpool, travel north on OH 11 for 5.45 miles to OH 7 north exit. Follow OH 7 north 2.98 miles to Leslie Road and turn right. Go 0.81 mile to the campground entrance on the right.

GPS COORDINATES: N40° 43.857' W80° 37.374'

6

⛺ Big Creek Park

Beauty ★★★ Privacy ★★★ Spaciousness ★★★★ Quiet ★★★★ Security ★★ Cleanliness ★★★

This little park offers a big dose of natural exploration opportunities.

What Big Creek Park lacks in size—only 644 acres—it makes up for in interaction with the natural environment of northeast Ohio. Several miles of hiking trails provide access to soak up the woodland environment. The park welcomes nature enthusiasts of all levels. The 0.7-mile Trillium Trail courses through forest that grows from seeds left by melting glaciers 10,000 years ago.

Located in the northern reaches of the park are Big Creek Park's four campsites. As campsites go, this is about as good as it gets, especially since the park lies in the middle of a light residential area. While walking to any of the sites, you soon forget that neighborhoods and grids of roads are less than a mile away. A gravel lane leads to a wide parking area, and a camping area sign displays the reservation schedule for that day and the next few—and takes the guesswork out of knowing which site is which and what is and is not allowed. The signage is well maintained, as are the ponds, sitting and wildlife-viewing areas, and the trails that traverse the park's intensely preserved natural surroundings.

Sites A and B are found by walking 20 yards into the oak-dominated forest. Site A is first. It's not difficult to select the spot for the tent, as there are two tent pads made of a timber frame and filled with a bed of bark mulch. The tent pads are approximately 12 x 16 feet and

A short walk leads to backcountry-style camping at Big Creek Park.

KEY INFORMATION

LOCATION: 9160 Robinson Road
Chardon, Ohio 44024

CONTACT: Operated by Geauga Park District:
440-286-9516, geaugaparkdistrict.org

OPEN: Year-round

SITES: 2 with tent pads, 2 with lean-tos

EACH SITE HAS: Fire ring, grill, picnic table,
firewood rack, lantern post

WHEELCHAIR ACCESS: Two trails, restrooms

ASSIGNMENT: Reservations must be made at
least 3 days in advance by calling 440-286-
9516 or online at geaugaparkdistrict.org

REGISTRATION: Permit must be kept on
person; printable permit online; permit at
Meyer Center located on Big Creek Park
grounds

AMENITIES: Pit toilets, water supply,
fishing lake

PARKING: In parking area; it's a 40-yard walk
to sites.

FEE: $5 for Geauga County residents,
$10 for nonresidents

ELEVATION: 1,119 feet

RESTRICTIONS

PETS: On leash only

FIRES: In fire ring

ALCOHOL: Prohibited

VEHICLES: In parking area only

OTHER: Camping by permit only; must be age
18 or older to obtain a permit; cutting trees
or gathering firewood is prohibited;
no cooking in stone fireplace structures

---

slightly raised above the ground to ensure a dry floor. The 8-foot-wide pathway to these sites is well packed, so using a small utility cart to carry in your gear will not be a problem. At the entrance to site A is a firewood rack with a raised bottom and covered roof. Firewood is not provided by the park system, but it's common for previous campers to leave leftover wood for the next camper. On the east edge of site A is access to a hiking trail. The site is spread out with no cramping of tent pad, picnic table, or fire ring.

Site B sits 20 yards farther back from site A. Its layout is similar to site A, with tent pads, a fire ring with grate, and two picnic tables. Painted on a large oak tree at site B are blue blazes, guiding hikers working the section of the Buckeye Trail that slips through Big Creek Park. The Buckeye Trail is a 1,444-mile hiking circuit of trails and roads that wind around Ohio, touching each corner of the state.

Sites C and D are accessed from the parking area using a separate path from A and B's pathway. Sites C and D don't have tent pads; instead, each site features a lean-to covered with cedar siding and roofing. The lean-tos have full sides and a raised, wooden floor, and their dimensions allow a small dome tent to be set up inside. Rising in front of each lean-to is a stone chimney with a fireplace that faces its interior. A few feet of open space on either side of the chimney allow campers access into the lean-to.

If you have time, definitely check out nearby Whitlam Woods. To get there, exit Big Creek Park and travel north 0.4 mile to Pearl Road and turn right. Follow Pearl Road 0.8 mile to the parking area and trailheads of Whitlam Woods. Deep ravines decorated with multiple species of ferns and flora that are only found in northern habitats thrive here in this special park. Huge hemlock, maple, and beech trees cover this 100-acre park, and a trail system gives entry to the mature forest that has escaped development over the last century. A photo-worthy trail descends to the cool bottom of a ravine and crosses a creek via a wooden footbridge. Pause on the bridge and study the creek for a glimpse of aquatic critters moving about the stones.

Big Creek Park

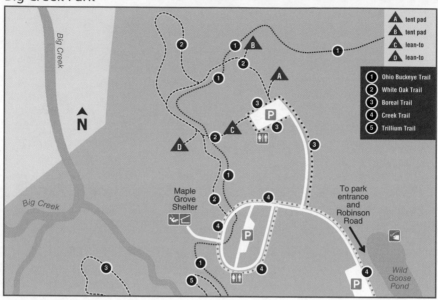

GETTING THERE

From I-90, take Exit 200 south of Painesville and go south on OH 44 for 3 miles to Clark Road. Turn left and travel east 1.8 miles to Robinson Road on the right. Follow Robinson Road south 0.9 mile to the park entrance on the right.

GPS COORDINATES: N41° 37.289' W81° 12.051'

7

⚕ Fernwood State Forest:
HIDDEN HOLLOW CAMPGROUND

Beauty ★★★ Privacy ★★★ Spaciousness ★★★ Quiet ★★★★ Security ★ Cleanliness ★★★

Fernwood State Forest features ridgetop camping in a well-managed forest.

The early settlers were met with steep hills and deep hollows covered with a heavy forest as they entered northeastern Ohio. Blazing trails for wagons filled with family and dreams of a new life was a test of wills. The area that holds Fernwood State Forest was one of the first to test the settlers. What was then a challenging wilderness is now a diverse and expansive landscape of woodlands with some meadows mixed in. The 3,032-acre state forest was once stripped of coal by surface mining. However, hundreds of acres were not touched by the massive shovels, and now those forest-covered ridges and bottoms have matured into a woodland recreational area—some trees are more than 100 years old. Not far from the Ohio River, the ridges and valleys under Fernwood are also evidence of the land-changing waters that flowed here thousands of years ago. Reforestation programs are ongoing, resulting in additional forest cover for generations to come.

Fernwood State Forest's woodlands call to those who cherish the forest environment. The mining activities left behind dozens of ponds flanked with high cliffs (watch your step when hiking off-trail) that now provide decent bass fishing. The forests are teeming with wildlife that is managed with ethical hunting seasons. Fernwood is a popular destination for

Lush campsites line the road at Fernwood State Forest.

LOCATION: 11 Township Road 181
Bloomingdale, Ohio 43910

CONTACT: 740-266-6021,
forestry.ohiodnr.gov/fernwood

OPEN: Year-round

SITES: 22 primitive

EACH SITE HAS: Fire ring, picnic table

WHEELCHAIR ACCESS: None

ASSIGNMENT: First come, first served

REGISTRATION: Campers must select a site,
then a forest officer will issue a permit.

AMENITIES: Pit toilet, wastewater disposal
basin, trash containers, water hand pump

PARKING: At each site

FEE: Free

ELEVATION: 1,180 feet

RESTRICTIONS

PETS: Permitted

FIRES: In fire ring

ALCOHOL: Prohibited

VEHICLES: 2/site

OTHER: Berries, nuts, and mushrooms
may be gathered and removed except
from tree seed orchards or posted areas.

anglers, hunters, and ATV enthusiasts. ATV riders are restricted to designated areas, which keeps things calm and quiet for those who prefer to explore on foot.

Fernwood State Forest consists of four sections, only a mile or so apart. Sitting on a ridgetop in the northern section is Hidden Hollow Campground. Although the ridgeline location and the campground's name place don't match, the hidden portion of the name is correct. A maintained paved road welcomes campers to this concealed campground. Don't let the first glimpse of site 1 mislead you into thinking the sites are small. They're not wide, but they are long, and each has a paved parking space. At the end of the parking space is where the campsite begins, tucked under shade trees and surrounded by wild shrubs and wildflowers. The picnic table, fire ring, and your tent will be hidden by your vehicle from the road. Each site is also divided by small trees and vegetation, which adds to the privacy.

The sites are situated along each side and around the cul-de-sac of the 0.25-mile campground road. Sites 3 and 4 offer the most solitude when the campground gets busy, but that is hardly ever the case. During deer-hunting season in October and November, this campground serves as a base camp for sportsmen roaming the state forest in search of Ohio's most sought-after game animal. At the end of the road, on the outside of the paved loop are sites 9, 10, and 11. These sites are not as deep as the first eight, but they do provide ample tent space to the side of the parking space. Inside the loop is a well-maintained and clean pit toilet. A bulletin board with a few maps of the forest is mounted to the front wall of the pit toilet.

Hiking through the forest is primarily off trail; however, there is a designated trail accessible between sites 17 and 18. At that same point is a water hand pump, with a warning sign that the water is for washing only, not for human consumption. The hiking trail (no horses permitted), called Fernwood Land Lab Trail, promotes continuing forest, soil, and water management practices that involve area schoolchildren annually.

For an impressive overlook of the forest region, jump in the car and drive from the campground back to County Road 26. From there, turn left (east) and travel 2.74 miles to the forest headquarters. Turn right on a service road and follow it 1.5 miles to a dead end with two scenic overlooks on the left. Near the end of this service road is a small picnic area that looks like a campground (it once was), but it isn't. The views from the overlooks are awesome, encompassing some of Ohio's most steep ridges and deepest ravines. After enjoying a picnic at one of the overlooks, return to CR 26, turn right, and descend more than 300 feet in less than 0.75 mile. Drive slowly and enjoy the view in front and to the side as you traverse the steep ravine you were just photographing a few moments earlier. At the end of CR 26, turn right and go to the next road on the left. This is Fernwood Road, and it leads to Wintersville, a medium-size town with plenty of retail sources to restock for the remainder of the camping trip.

Fernwood State Forest: Hidden Hollow Campground

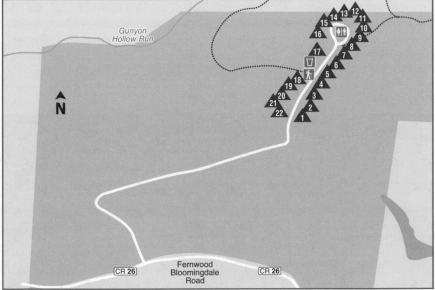

GETTING THERE

From Bloomingdale, follow CR 26 south 2.5 miles to where CR 26 and CR 25 converge. Turn left to stay on CR 26 for 0.7 mile. At the campground signage, turn left onto the forest road and travel 0.5 mile, then turn left into the campground.

GPS COORDINATES: N40° 19.863' W80° 45.966'

8

⛺ Findley State Park

Beauty ★★★ Privacy ★★ Spaciousness ★★ Quiet ★★ Security ★★★ Cleanliness ★★★

A pleasing, calm lake is the focal point of this forestland retreat.

Discovering forested Findley State Park among the level agricultural lands of north-central Ohio is a pleasant surprise. The park surrounds 93-acre Findley Lake, an electric-motors-only impoundment. Kayaking and canoeing the lake are the prime warm-weather pursuits, and for worthy reasons—wildlife, birdlife, lake coves, curvy shorelines, and a diversity of aqua vegetation decorate the lake. When snow blankets the park, hardy tent campers with cross-country skis find the forest and the manageable trails that weave through the heart of the park a wonderful place to be.

Entering the park through the main entrance from OH 58 gives visitors the feeling they are passing through a geographical portal. Take a right and travel south on Park Road 3 to find the

Paddling is a popular way to explore Findley Lake.

LOCATION: 25381 OH 58
Wellington, Ohio 44090-9010

CONTACT: 440-647-4490,
parks.ohiodnr.gov/findley

OPEN: Year-round; limited facilities, with water
behind maintenance building, in winter

SITES: 151 nonelectric (59 are walk-in),
91 electric

EACH SITE HAS: Picnic table, fire ring

WHEELCHAIR ACCESS: Sites 192 and 255–
257 and restrooms are ADA-accessible.

ASSIGNMENT: Walk-in sites first come, first
served; others may be reserved at 866-644-
6727 or ohiostateparks.reserveamerica.com

REGISTRATION: Self-registration station
at campground office, if campground
office closed

AMENITIES: Showers, flush toilets, laundry,
camp store, sports courts, playground,
swimming beach, boat rentals, disc-golf
course, nature center

PARKING: At each site

FEE: $26 nonelectric, $30 electric

ELEVATION: 914 feet

RESTRICTIONS

PETS: On leash only

QUIET HOURS: 10 p.m.–7 a.m.

FIRES: In fire ring, which must not be moved

ALCOHOL: Prohibited in public areas in every
state park but may be consumed within the
confines of a rented cabin, cabin site, lodge
room, or campsite

VEHICLES: 2/site

OTHER: Gathering firewood prohibited;
maximum 6 people/site; checkout is 1 p.m.;
minimum age to rent a campsite is 18.

campground, but not before passing through a challenging disc-golf course 0.25 mile south of the park entrance. A well-stocked camp office stands guard at the camp entrance.

To find the first come, first served sites (1–27), turn right past the camp office onto Park Road 6. This nonelectric section is the farthest from Findley Lake, the main attraction of Findley State Park. What this section does offer, however, is a stay deeper in the forest. Site 3 sits back a dozen yards from the park road, while most sites at this campground are at the road's edge. Sites 14 and 15 can accommodate a couple of camping families who want to interact but still appreciate a touch of privacy from neighboring sites. At the end of Park Road 6 is a cul-de-sac, with site 26 being the choice of the few sites on the outside of the turnaround. It's a roomy site with space for a family-size tent and plenty of elbow room for folks around the fire ring.

At the halfway point from Park Road 6 back to Park Road 3, on the right, is Park Road 8 and sites 36–64. These sites are all nonelectric, which discourages RVers from setting down the leveling jacks in this quiet section. Site 57 touches the turnaround with a parking pad but sprawls out wide under heavy tree canopy during the summer months and is sprinkled with orange and red leaves during fall. A couple of small tents will fit on this site nicely, as will a dining canopy. As Park Road 8 nears the intersection with Park Road 6, site 64 sits on the right and is wider than average with ample privacy on both sides.

Back to Park Road 3, turn right to find nonelectric sites 73–102. Although this section lies in the center of the campground, it still remains fairly quiet even during peak summer camping season. The 0.8-mile Spillway Trail passes through this section, leading hikers to the dam and a wide view of the lake—a perfect spot to watch the sun set. Also intersecting this section is the 0.5-mile Lake Trail, an easy walk with a senses-pleasing blend of forest and lake environment. As Park Road 3 returns to the main intersection, sites 106 and 107 on the right are heavily wooded with trees standing within several feet of each other, which creates a sense that you're off the beaten path. Just past these sites, turn right onto Park Road 11, where most of the sites are more open and receive direct sun most of the day. Although, site 130 is a pleasing tent spot where the forest juts out toward the road.

Park Roads 12 and 13 hold the electric sites, so RVs populate those two sections. Park Road 10 is a 0.2-mile road that leads to the campground boat ramp—an easy access point to launch the kayak. Sites 234–254 flank the road. Even though the boat ramp road sees some traffic, these roadside sites are decent tent sites with ample shade.

The 200-acre Wellington Wildlife Area is a western neighbor of the state park. Directly across OH 58, the wildlife area holds two small ponds for some quiet fishing. The property also has a healthy population of small game such as cottontail rabbits and pheasants for hunters. Songbirds pause here during spring migrations, so bring your bird identification guide. Parking and access to a wheelchair-accessible trail are located on Griggs Road, which connects with OH 58 between the state park's main entrance and the service-area entrance 0.7 mile south of the main entrance.

Findley State Park

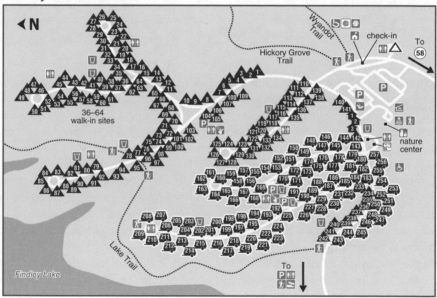

GETTING THERE

From Wellington, take OH 58 south 3 miles to the park entrance on the left. Follow Park Road 3 to the right (and signage) to the campground entrance.

GPS COORDINATES: N41° 07.401' W82° 12.344'

9

⛺ Harrison State Forest:
RONSHEIM CAMPGROUND

Beauty ★★ Privacy ★★★ Spaciousness ★★★ Quiet ★★★★ Security ★★ Cleanliness ★★

Explore hundreds of acres of mature woodlands at Harrison State Forest.

Harrison State Forest covers nearly 1,400 acres that was mined for coal in the late 1950s. When the State of Ohio purchased the land in 1961, a sustainable forest was the objective, and that goal has been reached. Within this remote forestland are ponds of various sizes and trees that have grown to mature status. The reforestation projects continue today, as the management plan put forth by the Division of Forestry was long-term. For outdoors enthusiasts, Harrison State Forest has grown into a rugged playground with miles of woodlands to explore.

There are two designated camping areas within the Harrison State Forest boundaries. One is an equestrian campground, and the other is Ronsheim Campground, a family camp. Ronsheim Campground consists of seven sites spread around the side of a rounded ridge like a displayed hand of playing cards. The paved lane that rolls through the campground seems out of place in such a remote campground, but because of the downslope of the grounds, the hard road is appreciated. Sites 1–6 are on the left, the low side of the hill, and are well spaced but a bit small. Site 4 has space for only a small tent. Site 7 is on the right side of the road, near the pit toilet. Campers must bring their own drinking water.

Allow an extra day or two to hike the woodlands at Harrison State Forest.

Photo courtesy of Ohio Department of Natural Resources

KEY INFORMATION

LOCATION: Toot Road
Cadiz, Ohio 43907

CONTACT: 740-266-6021 (Fernwood State Forest handles Harrison State Forest calls); forestry.ohiodnr.gov/harrison

OPEN: Year-round

SITES: 7 primitive

EACH SITE HAS: Fire ring, picnic table

WHEELCHAIR ACCESS: None

ASSIGNMENT: First come, first served

REGISTRATION: Forest officer will visit occupied sites and issue camping permit

AMENITIES: Pit toilet, wastewater disposal basin, trash containers

PARKING: At each site

FEE: Free

ELEVATION: 1,226 feet

RESTRICTIONS

PETS: Permitted

FIRES: In fire ring

ALCOHOL: Prohibited

VEHICLES: 2/site

OTHER: Berries, nuts, and mushrooms may be gathered and removed except from tree seed orchards or posted areas.

Across the road from site 7 is a trailhead identified with a brown sign displaying the word DAM. The trail descends 400 feet to a long but narrow, remote lake surrounded by forest, except for the dam. Pack a rod and reel and a few plastic worms to catch the evening's dinner. Largemouth bass averaging 2 pounds are common in these surface-mining reclamation ponds, which are numerous throughout northeastern Ohio.

Mounted on the front of the latrine building is a bulletin board. Information regarding camping at Harrison State Forest and Ohio's State Forest system is posted here. This campground doesn't offer any organized activities or programs, but is instead a quiet place to be enveloped by the forest and the sights and sounds thriving there. If you see a large bird with a red crown and black and white striped face, quickly flying from large tree to large tree, it may be Ohio's largest woodpecker, the Pileated Woodpecker. With the forest surrounding the campground, and without any residential buildings or homesteads nearby, the wildlife is relaxed and active year-round. It's your responsibility to blend in to take in the show.

September through October, the small campground is frequented by sportsmen. All of Harrison State Forest is an attraction to both hunters and anglers. There are a couple of sportsmen's clubs located on a neighboring road, but those wanting a serene camping experience will still have it. Open to the public, a shooting and archery range is available on Township Road 182, the neighboring road.

To get a good look at the forest's diversity, hit the trail. A series of marked hiking/bridle trails runs through the state forest. From the campground, return to the entrance of the campground and turn right on Toot Road. At 100 yards, you'll reach a parking area, which is used by equestrians for parking their trucks and trailers. A trail leads to the west and meanders for 0.9 mile before arriving at, and crossing, TR 182. For even more miles of trekking adventure, turn north on TR 182 and go past the gun range to a continuation of the hiking/bridle trail heading west for 1.1 miles to meet TR 186. Follow the trail across TR 186 and go 0.5 mile to the equestrian campground. The trail leads hikers and horses through pine and deciduous forests of various densities and skirts several ponds as well.

Harrison State Forest: Ronsheim Campground

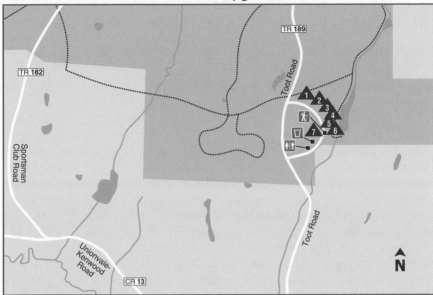

GETTING THERE

From Cadiz, follow OH 9 north 3.5 miles to CR 13 (Upper Clearfork Road). Turn right and travel 2.3 miles to TR 189 (Toot Road). Turn left and watch for a brown signpost with a tree symbol at the corner of CR 13 and Toot Road. Go 0.8 mile to the campground road on the right.

GPS COORDINATES: N40° 19.803' W80° 59.375'

10

⛺ Jefferson Lake State Park

Beauty ★★★ Privacy ★★★ Spaciousness ★★★ Quiet ★★★ Security ★★ Cleanliness ★★★

This small, hidden park in the Appalachian Highlands offers abundant recreation.

The hills and hollows that harbor Jefferson Lake State Park were the home of the Mingo leader Logan in the late 1700s. The broken topography provided efficient opportunities for hunting and navigating around the incoming settlers. Today, the 962-acre park is a quiet and peaceful place to recreate on land and water. In one of the park's valleys is the park's namesake, Jefferson Lake. The lake was constructed in 1934 as a project of the Civilian Conservation Corps, also known as Roosevelt's Tree Army. The lake is a beauty for paddling on a spring or fall day, when the surrounding forest is abundant with the sights and smells of nature. During summer, throw a blanket out on the 200-foot beach and take a swim after a picnic lunch.

Nearly 18 miles of trails meander throughout Jefferson Lake State Park. This park is favored by equestrians, who share the campground's 49 sites. There are plenty of trail options for both horse riders and hikers. The Campground Hikers Trail is 2 miles of foot traffic only. The Campground Horse Trail is a 3-mile bridle-only trail. Both trails explore the expanse of the ridge supporting the campground. Six additional trails, ranging from 1 mile

A mix of shaded and sunny sites is available at Jefferson Lake State Park.

KEY INFORMATION

LOCATION: 501 Township Road 261A
Richmond, Ohio 43944

CONTACT: 330-222-1712 (Guilford Lake
State Park handles Jefferson Lake calls);
parks.ohiodnr.gov/jeffersonlake

OPEN: Year-round; limited facilities in winter

SITES: 44 nonelectric, 5 electric

EACH SITE HAS: Picnic table, fire ring

WHEELCHAIR ACCESS: Pit toilets are
ADA-accessible.

ASSIGNMENT: Walk-in sites only, first-come,
first-served

REGISTRATION: Self-registration station at
campground entrance

AMENITIES: Pit toilets, water spigots, sports
courts, playground, swimming beach

PARKING: At each site

FEE: $20; deduct $3 in winter

ELEVATION: 1,210 feet

RESTRICTIONS

PETS: On leash only

QUIET HOURS: 10 p.m.–7 a.m.

FIRES: In fire ring, which must not
be moved

ALCOHOL: Prohibited in public areas in
every state park but may be consumed
within the confines of a rented cabin,
cabin site, lodge room, or campsite

VEHICLES: 2/site

OTHER: Gathering firewood prohibited;
maximum 6 people/site

to nearly 5 miles, cater to both hikers and equestrians. A trail map is posted at the entrance to the campground at the office.

The campground is laid out on a ridge above the lake, but the view of the lake is blocked by the forest. After registering at the camp office, the camp road leads uphill to the first sites flanking both sides of the road. A new, well-built pit toilet sits at the top of the first tier of the ridge, serving the first dozen sites. The road continues on toward the summit of the ridge as sites continue to flank the road. For the best tent sites, continue to the loop at the end of the camp road. The seven sites spread around the outside of the loop are well shaded and roomy. All of those sites are tent-friendly, and although they slope slightly, pitching a larger tent is manageable. Site 49 is my pick of the litter: It's the farthest from the others, has plenty of elbow room, is within a 1-minute walk of another new pit toilet, and has access to the Campground Hikers Trail at the rear of the site. Site 49 is nonelectric, so if you prefer juice, there are five electric sites at the center of the campground.

Back at the lake, the north shoreline provides easy access for anglers along the mowed picnic area. For anglers preferring to paddle to the opposite shoreline guarded by forest, a paved launch ramp makes launching a kayak a quick task. A public hunting area exists throughout the outer perimeters of the park. Turkey hunters in spring, as well as archery hunters in late fall in pursuit of Ohio's most plentiful game animal, the white-tailed deer, utilize the campground as a base camp. From late spring through early fall, however, the campground has plenty of vacancy. It's perfect for tent campers looking for a quiet night or two off the beaten path. To prove this point, reservations are not needed at Jefferson Lake campground; it is first come, first served with self-registration. On a weekday, you may just have the entire campground to yourself.

Jefferson Lake State Park

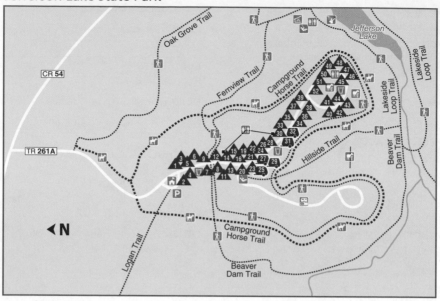

GETTING THERE

From Wintersville, follow OH 43 north 5.5 miles, through Richmond, to State Park Mooretown Road and turn right. Drive north 3.5 miles to Township Road 261A (Snow Wolf Road) and turn left. Travel south 0.5 mile to the campground entrance.

GPS COORDINATES: N40° 28.137' W80° 48.442'

11

⚑ Nimisila Reservoir Metro Park

Beauty ★★ Privacy ★★ Spaciousness ★★ Quiet ★★★ Security ★★ Cleanliness ★★

Camp among eight lakes and marshlands, and the hundreds of wildlife species thriving there.

The Nimisila Reservoir Metro Park campground sits on the Nimisila Peninsula, which is a neighbor of Portage Lakes State Park. The campground was operated by the ODNR Division of Parks and Watercraft until 2015, when Summit Metro Parks took the wheel. Founded in 1921, Summit Metro Parks (Summit County) is the second-oldest metro park system in Ohio, so they know how to manage a park well. Although it's situated within a few minutes' drive from Akron and Canton, the park holds urban sprawl at bay. If residents of northeast Ohio are short on time, the Nimisila campground offers a quick camping option. A mix of marshes and woodlands produces a diverse natural habitat that is special to Ohio.

The Nimisila Peninsula is a bird-watcher's paradise, from eagles and ospreys to warblers and purple martins. The purple martins perform quite an aerial show in August as they gather by the thousands in preparation for their migration south. Avid birders make a migration of their own to the Nimisila Peninsula to witness this impressive act of nature.

With so much natural splendor to observe, you'll need a quiet place to spend the night, and this small campground sitting on the peninsula in the middle of the Nimisila Reservoir fills the bill. The campground entrance is on the left before you reach the anglers' parking area (Lot C4 on Summit Metro Parks map). From this parking area, several hundred yards

Wildlife flourishes in the many lakes and marshes at Nimisila Reservoir Metro Park.

LOCATION: 5550 Christman Road
Akron, Ohio 44319

CONTACT: Operated by Summit Metro Parks:
330-867-5511 (Monday–Friday), 330-865-
8065 (weekends);summitmetroparks.org

OPEN: Year-round

SITES: 23 nonelectric, 6 electric

EACH SITE HAS: Fire ring, picnic table

WHEELCHAIR ACCESS: Sites 12, 14, and 18
(electric) are ADA-accessible

ASSIGNMENT: By reservation at
reserveamerica.com

REGISTRATION: Self-registration at
campground entrance station

AMENITIES: Pit toilet, sports courts, playground, boat ramp, firewood for sale Friday
and Saturday Memorial Day–Labor Day

PARKING: At each site

FEE: May–Oct.: nonelectric$25 weeknights,
$30 weekends;electric $30 weeknights,
$35 weekends; Nov.–Apr.: electric sites only,
$22.50

ELEVATION: 1,007 feet

RESTRICTIONS

PETS: On leash at all times

QUIET HOURS: 10 p.m.–6 a.m.

FIRES: In fire ring only

ALCOHOL: Prohibited

VEHICLES: 2/site, provided they are on paved
pad;overflow parking available

OTHER: Gathering firewood prohibited;
maximum 6 people/site; 10-night maximum
stay in a 30-day period

of shoreline are accessible for fishing or bird-watching. A small self-registration station stands at the campground gate, displaying posted information about the campground and the park. Since the park consists of several lakes and ponds—not all connected—having a map at hand is a must to find your way around.

After passing the campground information station, turn right to follow the one-way traffic pattern. Immediately on the right are sites 1 and 2, which are nearest to Nimisila Reservoir, the most southern lake of the Portage Lakes chain. As you round the corner, the reservoir will come into view through the few breaks in the forest. A mixed stand of pines and deciduous trees keeps the campground cool during the summer months.

A barricade lies straight ahead, which blocks the road through a section that held additional campsites when the state managed the campground. Turn left and follow the park road to the next set of campsites. Note that the elevation of the campground is not much above the water level of the reservoir. Throughout the campground are several low spots that can be somewhat marshy at times, but the campsites are not soggy. On the left are sites 3–7, which are situated to keep the park road between the campsites and the wetland of the Nimisila Reservoir. Don't be surprised if a Canada goose and a row of fuzzy goslings pass through these sites during breakfast on a spring camping trip. At Nimisila, you'll be one on one with the wild residents, which adds to the unique camping experience here.

After passing site 7, a boat ramp is on the right. As the road turns back toward the campground entrance, sites 8–29 sit among a mature pine woodlot. These sites are well spaced and flank both sides of the road. Although the campground is not in a remote forestland or miles away from any village, you'll have the sense of staying in an out-of-the-way place.

Nimisila Reservoir Metro Park

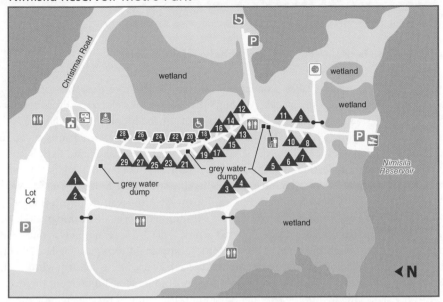

GETTING THERE

From I-77, take Exit 111 north of Canton and go west on Portage Street 4.7 miles to Lutz Avenue. Turn right and travel north on Lutz 2.1 miles to Mt. Pleasant Street. Turn right, and then make an immediate left onto Christman Road. Travel north 2.2 miles to the park entrance on the left.

GPS COORDINATES: N40° 56.561' W81° 31.250'

12

⚠ Punderson State Park

Beauty ★★ Privacy ★★ Spaciousness ★★ Quiet ★★ Security ★★★ Cleanliness ★★

Punderson Lake is the largest and deepest natural lake in Ohio.

One of Ohio's few natural lakes, Punderson Lake is a kettle lake that was formed by a remaining chunk of a receding glacier. Although the lake permits electric motors only, paddling is the preferred power source. The abundance of aquatic life skirting the lake's edges is best viewed from a gliding kayak. Throughout the park's surrounding woodlands, meadows, and marshes, wildlife, especially birds, is prevalent. Punderson Lake State Park is truly a four-season recreation destination. The park's central trail, the Huron Trail, is enjoyed by hikers in summer and by cross-country skiers when the snow falls. Since this park is smack in the middle of Ohio's snow belt, park visitors don't waste time waiting for summer.

Camping in the woods of Punderson Lake is a tradition of sorts. The campground overlays a former American Indian village. So what is now a place of recreation was once a life-sustaining site. Although the tents at Punderson's campground today are made of colored nylon and the fish sizzling in pans over campfires are a delicacy, being in touch with Mother Nature is still a necessity. Tents are a favored means of lodging at Punderson; the dozens of tent-only signs attached to the site-identification posts confirm this. Watch for the little signs displaying a tent symbol, which are found in every section of the campground.

The campground is basically split into two sections, northern and southern, and each offers a different flavor of camping style. The southern section rests at a lower elevation

Punderson State Park offers dozens of tent-only campsites.

KEY INFORMATION

LOCATION: 11755 Kinsman Road
Newbury, Ohio 44065

CONTACT: 440-564-2279,
440-564-1195 (seasonal camp office);
parks.ohiodnr.gov/punderson

OPEN: Year-round; only sites 1–90, with
shower house and water, open in winter

SITES: 12 nonelectric, 167 electric

EACH SITE HAS: Picnic table, fire ring

WHEELCHAIR ACCESS: No specific
ADA-accessible sites

ASSIGNMENT: Walk-in sites first come, first
served; others may be reserved at 866-644-
6727 or ohiostateparks.reserveamerica.com

REGISTRATION: Self-registration if campground office closed

AMENITIES: Showers, flush toilets, laundry,
sports courts, playground, swimming beach,
boat rentals, marina, disc-golf course,
18-hole golf course, archery range, lighted
sled hill and tow rope, bike rentals at
campground

PARKING: At each site

FEE: $22 nonelectric, $28 electric; deduct $3
in winter

ELEVATION: 1,154 feet

RESTRICTIONS

PETS: On leash only

QUIET HOURS: 10 p.m.–7 a.m.

FIRES: In fire ring

ALCOHOL: Prohibited

VEHICLES: 1/site unless a second can fit on
parking pad; $2/day for second vehicle

OTHER: Gathering firewood prohibited;
maximum 6 people/site; checkout is 1 p.m.;
juvenile campers must provide written
permission from parents to camp alone.

than its northern counterpart. From the campground office, turn right past the dump station. Pass the first sites and focus on sites 71 and 69 on the left at the road's end. These sites
require a 10-yard jaunt up a slope to reach them at the edge of a young woodlot. Back in the
car, turn left and you'll see sites 66 and 64 on the left, perched on the hill and with level tent
spots. Follow this road to another road with a dead end visible on the left. Stop at the dead
end, where a restroom is on the left, and off in the woods straight ahead are eight primitive sites. These sites sit at the base of a hill and can be a touch muddy during wet weather.
Picnic tables and fire rings accompany the sites, but they lack efficient space for a private
night of tent camping.

From the dead end, turn around and drive through the 40s sites. When you reach the
water treatment plant, turn right. Sites 15–26 are closest to Punderson Lake but elevated
above the shoreline. Site 19 offers the best piece of terra to place a tent and soak up the
natural lake's aroma being carried by the gentlest breeze. Because of the nearly parallel
angle to the road, site 19's parking pad serves as a privacy barrier when a vehicle occupies
it. Place two chairs between the tent and the edge of the lake bank, and share a relaxing
experience with a camping buddy.

To access the northern section, return to the campground office and follow the camp
road through sites 91–97. Parking for site 96 is along the road, but the site is on the peak of
a small hill, surrounded by several small trees and low vegetation. Sites 100–156 lie along an
ascending road to the highest point in the campground. Most are sunny and sloped. Back
down the hill, near site 99, the area with sites 156–201 has a few tent-camping gems. Sites
187 and 188 are deep, wooded sites with several feet of vegetation between them and the
next sites. The Erie Trail passes by these sites, offering a footpath to both Punderson Lake

and Stump Lake—both are great destinations to observe various species of waterfowl in action. Before you leave Punderson, the historic lodge is worth a visit.

Punderson State Park

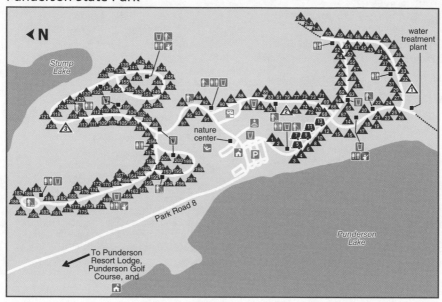

GETTING THERE

From Chardon, follow OH 44 south 7.6 miles to OH 87. Turn right on OH 87 and go 1.5 miles to the park entrance on the left.

GPS COORDINATES: N41° 27.367' W81° 12.334'

13

⛺ Tappan Lake

Beauty ★★ Privacy ★ Spaciousness ★★ Quiet ★★ Security ★★ Cleanliness ★★

Tappan Lake is an ideal summer lake getaway destination.

One of Muskingum Watershed Conservancy District's (MWCD) most scenic destinations, Tappan Lake offers an abundance of options to access its 2,350 water acres contained within 30 miles of shoreline. Rising above the shoreline are tall hills that support a thriving forest and a healthy population of wildlife. Multiple hiking trails rove those hills; check out the 4-mile Deer Trail that begins and ends at the amphitheater near the seasonal campground boat launch. If boating is not on the schedule, then additional hiking awaits. Located on the shore of Tappan Lake is the Buckeye Trail Association Century Barn, which serves as a hub for trail users. The 1,440-mile Buckeye Trail is a multiuse trail system that loops around the state.

The MWCD was organized in 1933 to manage the Muskingum River Watershed, which covers around 8,000 square miles in Ohio. In 2010, interest from petroleum companies in oil and natural gas deposits beneath eastern Ohio brought a substantial amount of land lease money to landowners and managers that sit on top of those resources. The MWCD is one of those entities experiencing the financial gains, and it developed a plan to invest in its parks by renovating infrastructure over the next couple of decades. As of 2019, camp-grounds of the MWCD parks were seeing upgraded sites, camper facilities, and construc-tion for additional camping opportunities. Although the MWCD parks are updating the

Tappan Lake is one of northeast Ohio's prettiest.

KEY INFORMATION

LOCATION: 84000 Mallarnee Road Deersville, Ohio 44693

CONTACT: Operated by Muskingum Watershed Conservancy District: 740-922-3649, tappanlakeohio.org

OPEN: Year-round; shower house open in winter

SITES: 550 electric

EACH SITE HAS: Fire ring, picnic table

WHEELCHAIR ACCESS: Shower and restroom are ADA-accessible

ASSIGNMENT: First come, first served and by reservation at 740-922-3649 or tappanlakeohio.org

REGISTRATION: Campground entrance station and online

AMENITIES: Camp store, pit toilets, drinking water, boat ramp, boat rentals, swimming beach, activity center, nature center

PARKING: At each site

FEE: $30 Apr.–Oct., $25 Nov.–Mar.

ELEVATION: 915 feet

RESTRICTIONS

PETS: Must be registered as campsite occupant; on leash no longer than 6 feet

QUIET HOURS: 11 p.m.–7 a.m.

FIRES: In fire ring

ALCOHOL: Allowed, but not publicly

VEHICLES: 2/site

OTHER: Must be age 18 and older to obtain a camping permit; checkout is 4 p.m.; gathering of fallen tree limbs for firewood allowed

campgrounds to accommodate the power demands of new, bigger RVs, tent campers still have a place here. A couple of new primitive camps are in the current plans, so be sure to ask about future tent-camping sections when making reservations.

After entering the park, two large campground sections on the left are populated by seasonal campers. Bypass those and follow the park road to the right to find three small campground sections resting in two pine groves and on a ridge above the southern lagoon of Tappan Lake. Not far from the beach is the first of two newly renovated, full-hookup camp areas featuring 50-amp power and concrete pads. While RVers populate these areas during the weekends and holidays, quiet tent camping is possible during the week.

But the ridgetop sections are the best for tenters. The first of those three sections rests at a lower elevation than the other two sections. Well-displayed signage directs campers to these campgrounds with ease. Driving along the park road that follows the outer edge of the wide valley, section one is on the right at the head of the valley. A small shelter house and drinking water spigot are on the left. The sites flank both sides of the paved road that ends with a tight loop with sites skirting its edge. The sites on the right going in have a small drainage ditch at the rear. Kids may find a few crawdads clambering in and out of den holes in that little channel.

Return to the main park road and turn right. Around the bend is the second section that is a bit higher and drier, but the sites are shorter. There is sufficient space between sites, but another drainage ditch and a rapidly ascending hillside keep this section situated close to the road. Pines tower over most of this section, as they do in the first area, but the surrounding vegetation is much denser here. Be sure to pack an ample supply of insect repellent. This second section is also laid out on both sides of a dead-end road. On the left side of the road, as you approach the loop, are four sites (912, 913, 914, and 915) grouped together in a small clearing in the pine forest. They're perfect for a group of friends or an extended family camping together. At the campground entrance is a shower building complete with laundry facilities and a drinking water spigot.

Leave the second section and continue up the hill on the main park road 0.45 mile to find the next camp, on the left. At the top of a ridge overlooking the lake is the Class B campground that provides electric to all of its 23 sites. These sites are conducive for tent camping, but small pop-up and hard-sided RVs also use these sites occasionally. This section sits in a partial clearing with sites lining each side of the road. The road courses along the center of the ridge and ends at another turnaround. Just short of the cul-de-sac is a pit toilet, a drinking-water fountain, and a dishwater disposal basin. The road takes a slight turn around a shallow, wooded ravine, which gives the next site, site 711, more privacy than any other in the campground. Site 711 sits among the trees but not among other campers.

Take a morning walk from Class B campground's entrance to the trailhead on the other side of the park road. The Turkey Ridge Trail, a 1.5-mile hiking trail that leads to the Tappan Wetland Wildlife Area, was developed by the National Campers and Hikers Association. Once at the observation station, listen and look for various waterfowl preparing to land through the fog rising off the lake's warm water. Later, mount a bike for an easy ride to the sandy beach or grab an ice cream cone at the camp store near the seasonal campground entrance.

Tappan Lake Campground

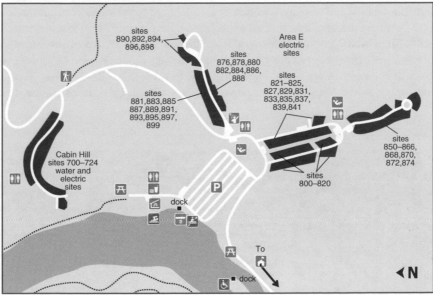

GETTING THERE

From Uhrichsville, follow OH 250 east a little over 14 miles to County Road 55 (Deersville Road) and turn right. Travel 3.7 miles to the park entrance on the right.

GPS COORDINATES: N40° 19.139' W81° 10.708'

14

⛺ West Branch State Park

Beauty ★★ Privacy ★★ Spaciousness ★★ Quiet ★ Security ★★★★ Cleanliness ★★

Lake views and shoreline camping are the attractions here.

Boaters who prefer to camp are attracted to West Branch State Park and its Michael J. Kirwan Lake. The 2,650-acre lake stretches over 7 miles, and its shoreline snakes around leaving an abundance of forks and coves, which are perfect for boating and angling. Boating is the thing to do here, but if you've had enough lake action, and still have some energy left, the park's 14 miles of hiking trails should polish off the day. A portion of the statewide Buckeye Trail passes through the park, including a 2-mile spur trail.

The lakeside camping here is first class and is popular with campers who want to fish or dangle their feet in the water only a few steps from their campsite. West Branch's campground is spread out on a branched peninsula—four smaller peninsulas of various sizes joined together. Most of the campground is kept cool by mature deciduous trees. This popular campground receives a blend of visitors, and although it's busy, a few lakeside sites offer a quiet retreat. The smallest and least-busy section is also anchored to the smallest peninsula, which rises 30 feet above the lake. Take the first right past the campground office to find this section. Sites 8–17 have wide views of the lake and are well shaded. Sites 12 and 14 have steep stone footpaths down to the water. At night, this section of the lake produces good catfishing action.

Back at the main campground road, turn right to access sites 34–76. Sites 52 and 56 have broad views of the reservoir and access to the lake as well. This stretch of lakeside sites

These lakeside sites provide plenty of shade.

KEY INFORMATION

LOCATION: 5570 Esworthy Road
Ravenna, Ohio 44266-9659

CONTACT: 330-269-3239,
parks.ohiodnr.gov/westbranch

OPEN: Year-round; in winter only sites 1–32
and shower house 1 open

SITES: 14 nonelectric, 155 electric

EACH SITE HAS: Picnic table, fire ring

WHEELCHAIR ACCESS: Sites 23, 39, 98, and
150 are ADA-accessible.

ASSIGNMENT: Walk-in sites first come, first
served; others may be reserved at 866-644-
6727 or ohiostateparks.reserveamerica.com

REGISTRATION: At camp office; self-
registration station on front of camp office

AMENITIES: Showers, flush toilets, laundry,
sports courts, playground, swimming beach
near site 160, boat rentals, marina

PARKING: At each site

FEE: $26 nonelectric, $30 electric;
deduct $3 in winter

ELEVATION: 1,013 feet

RESTRICTIONS

PETS: On leash only

QUIET HOURS: 10 p.m.–7 a.m.

FIRES: In fire ring, which must not be moved

ALCOHOL: Prohibited in public areas in every
state park but may be consumed within the
confines of a rented cabin, cabin site, lodge
room, or campsite

VEHICLES: 2/site

OTHER: Gathering firewood prohibited;
maximum 6 people/site

---

is popular with RVs, but there's ample space between sites, and the focus on the lakeview allows tent campers to find tranquility here. At the tip of this long peninsula are sites 62 and 64, which are spacious and situated at the mouth of a lake cove. Site 62 slopes away from the road and down 20 yards to a bench that invites a tent to be pitched there. A few steps more and you reach a gravel shoreline perfect for launching a kayak or canoe. Just be sure to paddle early in the morning before the motor boaters rough up the lake's surface. Lakeside site 39 is wheelchair-accessible and across the lane from a heated shower house.

The central section of the divided peninsula is covered with sites 77–127. This segment includes several full-hookup sites for large RVs and is active with campers strolling and biking. Avoid this area and head for the northwest peninsula branch, which includes sites 128–186. The nonelectric loop, with sites 133–145, is mostly sunny and void of any views. Bypass that loop and head for the two loops to the north. The loop with sites 150–170 is separated from the bustling center of the campground. Site 160 is the site to behold—the best lakeside spot in the campground. The elevation is only a few feet different from the site to the lake. It offers a 180-degree view of the lake, and with a buffer of vegetation and trees flanking both sides of the site, you'll feel as if you have the place to yourself. Just around the corner from site 160 is a small, sandy beach.

A quiet loop next to the last one hosts sites 171–186. Sites 180, 182, and 183 are also near the water's edge, at the mouth of a shallow cove with a view of the boat ramp on the opposite side. These sites are less roomy but adequate for peaceful tent camping. After exiting that loop and heading toward the campground office, you'll find a row of sites along a separate lane worthy of consideration. Sites 187–198 include a few spots on the edge of a lake cove. Of those, site 193 provides the most solitude and best location for a shore lunch. Good numbers of crappie and walleye populate Michael J. Kirwan Lake and are available for filling the menu.

West Branch State Park

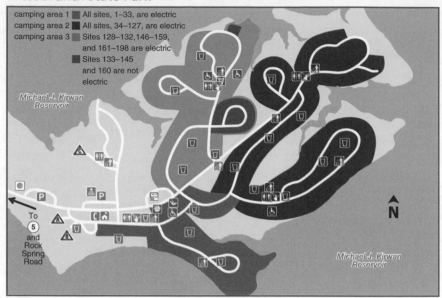

camping area 1 ■ All sites, 1–33, are electric
camping area 2 ■ All sites, 34–127, are electric
camping area 3 ■ Sites 128–132,146–159, and 161–198 are electric
■ Sites 133–145 and 160 are not electric

Michael J. Kirwan Reservoir

Michael J. Kirwan Reservoir

To 5 and Rock Spring Road

N

GETTING THERE

From I-76, take Exit 38 south of Ravenna and travel north on OH 44 for 4.4 miles to where OH 44 blends into OH 5. Follow OH 5 for 3 miles east to Rock Spring Road and turn right. Travel 0.3 mile to the park entrance on the left, and then follow signs to the campground office.

GPS COORDINATES: N41° 08.652' W81° 07.787'

SOUTHEAST

The American Electric Power campgrounds are some of the best in the state (see page 56).

15

⛺ American Electric Power (AEP) Recreation Land

CAMPGROUND K (Bicentennial): Beauty ★★★ Privacy ★★★ Spaciousness ★★★★ Quiet ★★★ Security ★★ Cleanliness ★★★

CAMPGROUND H (Wood Grove): Beauty ★★ Privacy ★★ Spaciousness ★★ Quiet ★★ Security ★★ Cleanliness ★★★

CAMPGROUND D (Sawmill Road): Beauty ★★ Privacy ★★ Spaciousness ★★ Quiet ★★ Security ★★ Cleanliness ★★★

CAMPGROUND A (Hook Lake): Beauty ★★★ Privacy ★★ Spaciousness ★★★ Quiet ★★★ Security ★★ Cleanliness ★★★★

These four remote campgrounds feature thousands of water acres for paddling and abundant wildlife.

The giant rusty bucket of the huge dragline named the Big Muskie is the only remaining remnant of the massive machine that extracted coal from southeastern Ohio's surface beginning in 1969. Today, 50,000 acres of those reclaimed mining lands, named the American Electric Power Recreation Land (AEPRL), provide outdoors enthusiasts with a plethora of adventures. The lands feature more than 350 ponds and lakes, a mix of deciduous and evergreen forests, rolling plains, and four campgrounds offering a variety of tent-camping scenarios. Although two interstate highways are within a short drive east and north, the AEPRL is one of Ohio's most remote camping destinations.

Driving south on OH 83 from Cumberland, turn east onto Township Road 13 and you'll first encounter Campground K. The drive alone quickly shakes the hustle-and-bustle

Everyone has access to fish AEPRL's 350 ponds.

KEY INFORMATION

LOCATION: McConnelsville

CONTACT: Operated by American Electric Power and Ohio Department of Natural Resources: 740-962-1205, aep.com/recreation/areas/recreationland

OPEN: Campgrounds D and K close in mid-December; Campgrounds A and H close around January 1. All reopen for the season in mid- to late April, weather permitting.

SITES: 176; overflow camping is permitted alongside designated sites within campgrounds

EACH SITE HAS: Picnic table, fire ring, trash can

WHEELCHAIR ACCESS: No specific ADA-accessible sites

ASSIGNMENT: First come, first served, but must obtain a free AEP Recreation Land Permit by calling the number above, 614-716-1000, or online at aep.com/recreation/areas/recreationland.

REGISTRATION: At all campground entrance stations

AMENITIES: Pit toilets, potable water stations (hand pumps), information stations, archery range

PARKING: At each site

FEE: Free, but must have AEP Recreation Land Permit in possession

ELEVATION:
Campground K: 866 feet
Campground H: 763 feet
Campground D: 831 feet
Campground A: 889 feet

RESTRICTIONS

PETS: On leash only

FIRES: In fire ring

ALCOHOL: Prohibited

VEHICLES: No limits

OTHER: No cutting of live trees for firewood, but deadwood on the ground may be used. Wading, bathing, and swimming are prohibited. No camp store, but supplies are available in Cumberland and McConnelsville.

feelings of a busy lifestyle as the rolling and rugged lands appear. The huge, colorful campground sign (all of the AEPRL campgrounds have these signs) is on the left. Turn left and follow the gravel road to and through the campground. The self-registration station is on the right. Once in the campground, a few sites are in the open on the right and offer plenty of space for multiple tents. (Note that none of the campsites in the AEPRL campgrounds are numbered.) The only pit toilet is also on the right.

After reaching the most northern point of Campground K, the road turns west, then south, and follows the shoreline of a beautiful, long, narrow lake. A potable water pump is available here. The first three campsites along the lake provide no shade, but access to the lake is only steps away. There's plenty of elbowroom, about 50 feet, between the lake sites. Fishing in the AEPRL is popular year-round, especially for bass. Be sure to include a heavy test line in your reel before casting to these largemouths, which regularly weigh over 4 pounds. Before the bottom lake road reconnects to the entry road, two sites on the right are set back in a woodlot but still offer easy access to the lake.

Back at the Campground K sign on TR 13, turn right and return to OH 83. To visit Campground H, turn south on OH 83 and go 1.4 miles to County Road 27. Turn left and travel 2.6 miles to Campground H on the right. You will cross over Dyes Fork on CR 27 before turning into the campground. This creek flows through the campground, offering kids the opportunity to flip over a few rocks in search of aqua critters. Soon after entering the campground, a group of eight sites are bordered by the entry and exit gravel lanes. These sites are heavily shaded and level, with a pit toilet available a few steps across

The Buckeye Trail is just one recreational opportunity for campers here.

the lane. Then, on the right, and as the lane leads into a woodgrove, the sites are closer together, but all are creekside. The woodgrove imparts a sense of tranquility, even with sites only 20 feet apart. The 16 sites along the creek are level, with space available for a small tent. Across the lane from the creekside sites are five level sites. A tent-only site (the only site on the right as the exit lane nears CR 27) is fairly open with shade on two sides. A camp host typically remains on site in spring, summer, and fall.

A short walk southeast from the campground's entrance on CR 27 leads to the Buckeye Trail, the 1,444-mile hiking trail that meanders around Ohio. At first, the trail was envisioned as leading from the Ohio River to Lake Erie, but it has evolved into a path through Ohio's geographic diversity. The Buckeye Trail utilizes county roads, unoccupied railroads, farmlands, and remote forests, such as the section that snakes through the AEPRL. The AEPRL section of the Buckeye Trail provides access to roadless areas, but be careful, as hundreds of high walls (cliffs) remain from the mining operations. Some of these have a drop of 50 feet or more, so it's important to stay on designated trails. Follow the blue blazes on trees and signposts.

To find Campground D, follow CR 27 back to OH 83. Be sure to make a short stop at the small park next to the AEPRL maintenance headquarters, where you'll find a scenic overlook and information about the AEPRL reclamation efforts and successes, as well as a description of the history of the scene across this wide valley. You may also have some cell phone service at this spot, as the elevation is 1,047 feet, one of the highest points in the area. After your stop at the park, travel south on OH 83 for 0.66 mile to the Campground D sign and access lane, which dead-ends at the campground. As you approach the main area of the campground, a few sites on the right offer secluded camping among young shade trees. A bit farther, on the left, is a volleyball court and swings with two sites nearby. Taking the right fork in the lane leads to wide, level sites on the left and a covered bridge on the right. The covered bridge is for foot traffic only and leads to a few secluded sites less than 50 yards from the bridge.

The second section of Campground D is uphill through a pine forest with sites on both sides of the lane. All sites are tent-friendly, especially the ones on the right. At the top of the hill, you'll find a supply of sawmill slabs cut into sections for firewood, free for the taking. The lane turns back toward the camp entrance at the firewood center, passing a shelter house and camp host site on the way out. Two ponds await anglers and wildlife-watchers a short walk west of the covered bridge.

Back at OH 83, turn left and go 1.7 miles to Campground A, one of the largest of the four AEPRL campgrounds and possibly the nicest. The main attraction here is Hook Lake, which is off-limits to anglers ages 16 and under. The lake is occasionally stocked with bass by conservation clubs and the ODNR's Division of Wildlife. Campground A also has a large, modern shelter house that hosts several events during the year. During those times and holidays, Campground A gets busy, but otherwise the AEPRL campgrounds are slightly used. The southern section of Campground A is attractive to group campers such as Boy Scouts. Those sites are open with very little shade but are spaced well apart, with more than 50 feet between them. In Campground A's northern section, sites are much smaller but situated in a forest surrounding three sides of Hook Lake. A few sites offer a narrow view of the lake. The lane leading through the northern section begins and ends near the campground entrance. The best sites to accommodate tents are on the left side of that looping lane.

Whether you want to fish, hike, or simply view wildlife, it's all available at AEPRL. As you travel about the area, take it slow because wildlife is abundant and regularly makes appearances—both on the road and at the campgrounds. You may even see a buffalo or zebra. OK, maybe not crossing next to your tent, but those animals do exist at The Wilds, a wildlife-conservation facility dedicated to rare and endangered species located just north of the campgrounds. The 10,000-acre center is the home of scientific studies and preservation practices of numerous species. Guided tours are available May–October. To visit The Wilds from Campground A, drive west, crossing OH 83, and follow the stone access road. After about 1 mile, Jesse Owens State Park is on the right; don't turn in, but continue across a lake dam, turn right on OH 284, and follow it north 8 miles to International Road. Turn right and go 1 mile to The Wilds parking lot.

Note: Jesse Owens State Park was previously an AEP campground, and the State of Ohio has plans to purchase more of the AEPRL in the future.

American Electric Power Recreation Land

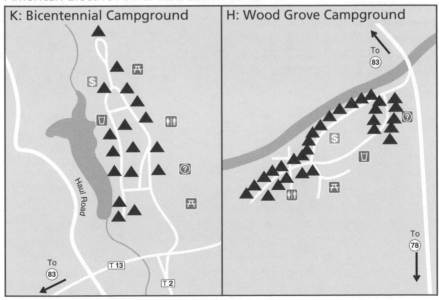

American Electric Power Recreation Land

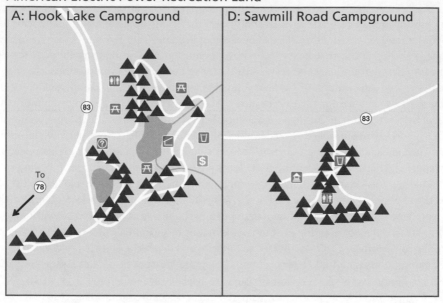

A: Hook Lake Campground   D: Sawmill Road Campground

GETTING THERE

From I-70, take Exit 169 and go south on OH 83 for 11.4 miles to Cumberland. Continue on OH 83 south 6.6 miles to TR 13. Turn left and follow TR 13 for 1.3 miles to the Campground K entrance road on the left.

GPS COORDINATES
Campground K: N39° 46.198' W81° 38.414'
Campground H: N39° 43.282' W81° 40.202'
Campground D: N39° 44.673' W81° 41.477'
Campground A: N39° 43.672' W81° 42.478'

16

⛺ Barkcamp State Park

Beauty ★★★ Privacy ★★ Spaciousness ★★★ Quiet ★★ Security ★★★★ Cleanliness ★★★★

This friendly park is one of eastern Ohio's best and is worthy of multiple visits.

The hills of Belmont County were frequented by settlers during the early 1800s, and many times their presence caused conflicts with the American Indians, who treasured their land, and rightly so. Today, the beauty of the region and the bounty of natural resources still exist, and it's evident why so many people wanted to claim this region as their own. After the settlers became regular inhabitants of the then heavily forested area, logging became a lucrative business and a necessity for the newcomers to set roots in the wild land. Barkcamp State Park gets its name from the de-barking facility that prepared logs for transport here a century ago. Inside the campground is a display of those pioneer days, complete with a variety of buildings and antique implements. The paved Pioneer Hiking Trail guides visitors through the collection of historical pieces. This trail is wheelchair-accessible, as are the showers and restrooms of the campground. Pausing next to the hand-hewn log cabin with a horse-drawn wagon parked next to it, it's easy to imagine the past. Interpretive signs placed around the pioneer displays reveal some interesting facts. The park has received several awards for its cleanliness and the staff's dedication to delivering exceptional service.

The focal point of the park is 117-acre Belmont Lake, which allows electric motors only. Of course, paddling is allowed and recommended. To find the boat ramp, turn right out of

Placid Belmont Lake is very canoe-friendly.

KEY INFORMATION

LOCATION: 65330 Barkcamp Park Road Belmont, Ohio 43718-9733

CONTACT: 740-484-4064, parks.ohiodnr.gov/barkcamp

OPEN: Year-round, including shower house and drinking water

SITES: 120 electric, 27 equestrian sites

EACH SITE HAS: Picnic table, fire ring

WHEELCHAIR ACCESS: Restrooms, shower house, and sites 15, 89, 138, and 143 are ADA-accessible.

ASSIGNMENT: Walk-in sites first come, first served; others may be reserved at 866-644-6727 or ohiostateparks.reserveamerica.com

REGISTRATION: At camp office; self-registration station on front of camp office

AMENITIES: Showers, flush toilets, laundry, playground, sports courts, boat ramp, boat rental, nature center, minigolf, archery range

PARKING: At each site, except for tent-only sites that have parking area

FEE: Apr. 1–Oct. 31, $26; Nov. 1–Mar. 31, $23; $1 less Sunday–Thursday; $2 more during holidays

ELEVATION: 1,225 feet

RESTRICTIONS

PETS: Allowed at sites 1–99 and on leash only

QUIET HOURS: 10 p.m.–7 a.m.

FIRES: In fire ring, which must not be moved

ALCOHOL: Prohibited in public areas in every state park but may be consumed within the confines of a rented cabin, cabin site, lodge room, or campsite

VEHICLES: 2/site

OTHER: Gathering firewood prohibited; 14-day stay limit; maximum 6 people/site; parking on grass prohibited; major supplies available in St. Clairsville

the campground and follow the signs. The view of the lake on the right is worthy of a quick stop to capture a photo before unloading your kayak. If you left your kayak or canoe at home, both types of watercraft are available for rent.

The first groups of sites you see after entering the campground are often used by RVers, and the equestrian sites are in a loop on the right. Tents are welcome on these sites, but the best tent sites are yet to come. Continue on the main road to camping area C. At the end of the road in camping area C is the tent area, with sites 122–134. These sites are evenly spaced around the base of a round knoll approximately 50 yards in diameter. A few small trees are sparingly located around the knoll. The sites are laid out in a loop like a circle of wagons gathered in defense mode, with a young forest and a carpet of underbrush as the backdrop. Sites 125 and 131 give the most privacy to tent campers, as they are the farthest from the parking area. A restroom and drinking water spigot are located two sites away from the tent area on the main campground road. A connecting trail leaves the campground at the tent area and leads to a bridle/snowmobile trail that parallels the lake's shoreline and length of the entire campground. Though Barkcamp's hiking trails are short and total less than 4 miles, equestrian trails meander for more than 30 miles. Take one of the bridle trails for a trek on foot, but watch your step for spent horse fuel.

A special forest not far from the park is a must-see. Dysart Woods is a 50-acre tract of old-growth oak forest and the largest known remnant of the original forest of southeastern Ohio. Some of the trees here are more than 300 years old and stand 140 feet tall. The property is managed and studied by Ohio University. Two foot trails wind through the old forest for visitors to explore, but do not touch or disturb the extraordinary natural environment. To find Dysart Woods, return to Township Road 92 and turn left. Drive 1.4 miles to OH 149 and turn right. Go 0.73 mile to OH 147 and turn left (south). Follow OH 147 for 4.79 miles to a wooden DYSART WOODS sign on the right. A rustic restroom is located next to the white farmhouse on the left, and parking is at the trailheads.

Barkcamp State Park

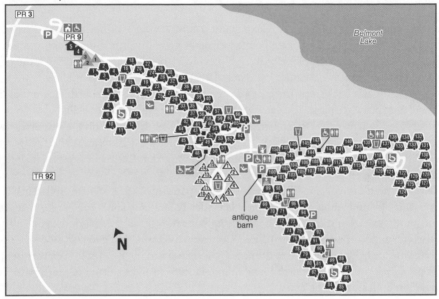

GETTING THERE

From I-70, take Exit 208 and go south on OH 149 for 0.8 mile. Turn left on TR 92 and drive 0.9 mile to the park entrance on the left. After entering the park, take an immediate right to reach the campground entrance.

GPS COORDINATES: N40° 02.780′ W81° 01.767′

17

⛺ Blue Rock State Park

Beauty ★★★ Privacy ★★ Spaciousness ★★ Quiet ★★★ Security ★★ Cleanliness ★★★

Campers will find plenty of nature and tranquility at this small state park.

The drive to the park on OH 60 is relaxing and scenic. A couple of miles before arriving at the park's entrance, Blue Rock State Forest welcomes you. Towering pines close to the road blend with deciduous forest plots, creating a patchwork of colorful woodlands. At the park, the forest opens up to reveal Cutler Lake, only 15 acres but overflowing with beauty with the towering forest as a backdrop. The lake was created in 1938 and remains the feature of this 322-acre gem of a state park. The dam was rebuilt in 2018 and the lake refilled.

Blue Rock State Park has two primary campgrounds, both located on the western side of the lake. The northern campground, with 47 sites, lies below the lake's dam, and the spillway creek flows through the heart of it. The southern campground, with 49 sites, is situated on a ridge with some sites overlooking the lake.

The northern campground drive has a one-way pattern. Sites 51–56 are circled in a loop on the right. Behind and above these sites is Cutler Lake Road; some road noise may steer you to another site, but the traffic is normally light. At the entrance to this loop, you will find a bathroom and pay phone. Following the one-way, paved lane, you'll find sites 59–64 along the creek near a bridge that crosses the creek to a visitor parking lot. These six sites offer the most privacy for tent campers. The lane then follows a straight stretch of creek with sites situated on both sides of the lane.

On the opposite side of the creek, another bridge leads to three rent-a-camps (sites with a tent set on a wooden platform with a lantern, sleeping pads, a cooler, and a camp stove, all

Sites at Blue Rock State Park provide direct access to the state forest.

KEY INFORMATION

LOCATION: 7924 Cutler Lake Road
Blue Rock, Ohio 43720-9728

CONTACT: 740-453-4377 or 740-674-4794
(in season), parks.ohiodnr.gov/bluerock

OPEN: March 28–December 4

SITES: 77 nonelectric; 21 nonelectric are
equestrian friendly

EACH SITE HAS: Picnic table, fire ring

WHEELCHAIR ACCESS: No specific
ADA-accessible sites

ASSIGNMENT: Walk-in sites first come, first
served; others may be reserved at 866-644-
6727 or ohiostateparks.reserveamerica.com

REGISTRATION: At camp store; check-in after
3 p.m., checkout at 1 p.m.

AMENITIES: Camp store with showers, flush
toilets, boat launch, boat rentals, swimming
beach, volleyball, basketball, archery range

PARKING: At each site

FEE: $20 weekends, $17 weekdays

ELEVATION: 847 feet

RESTRICTIONS

PETS: On leash only

QUIET HOURS: 10 p.m.–7 a.m.

FIRES: In fire ring

ALCOHOL: Prohibited

VEHICLES: 2/site; no parking on grass

OTHER: No visitors after 10 p.m.;
gathering firewood prohibited;
maximum 6 people/site

provided by the park) and five additional creek sites, although these sites are small with no space for a large tent. Back on the main lane, another small bridge on the right leads to the group camp area. A hiking trail is accessible at the forest edge behind the group camp's central fire ring. This trail leads to the southern campground and is a leg of the park's nature-filled, 0.6-mile Ruffed Grouse Trail. A footpath allows easy walking from the eastern edge of the northern campground to the camp store and shower house.

To access the southern campground, leave the northern campground's entrance and go north on Cutler Lake Road 0.1 mile to Corns Road on the left. Take Corns Road 0.15 mile to the campground entrance on the left. After passing the information station, campsites flank both sides of the park road. These sites, and the others leading to the loop overlooking the lake, are considered equestrian sites and offer no view of the lake. As the lane makes the turn at the ridge's edge that overlooks the lake, sites 21–25 have wooden decks overlooking the lake. Treetops obstruct a clear view of the water during leafy months, but autumn brings spectacular displays. These five sites are not big and can accommodate only a small tent. The nearest sites to the ridge's edge that offer plenty of tent-pitching space are sites 26–29. These spots are also a short walk to the restroom and the 0.4-mile Ground Cedar Trail, which leads to the 0.5-mile Vista Trail.

At the opposite end of the lake is a pack-in campground. To reach it, park in the lot on Cutler Lake Road that is 0.4 mile east of the camp store. From the parking lot, walk across the road bridge and past the first mowed path on the right. Continue on the road for 50 yards to a second mowed path and signage pointing the way to the pack-in sites and the Ruffed Grouse Nature Trail. The trail is all uphill, but the tranquil setting of the two-site campground is worth the effort to get there. A pit toilet, picnic table, and fire rings await campers looking for a backpacking-type experience.

Blue Rock State Forest surrounds the state park with 4,573 acres for exploring. Hiking and equestrian trails roam the creek bottoms and the steep forested hills flanking the waterways. Wildflowers, such as trilliums and cardinal flowers, as well as mosses and ferns, have a strong presence in and around the forest. The 0.8-mile Hollow Rock Trail, which parallels the southern shoreline of Cutler Lake, leads to photographic views of the lake and an abundance of songbirds and butterflies flittering about.

Blue Rock State Park

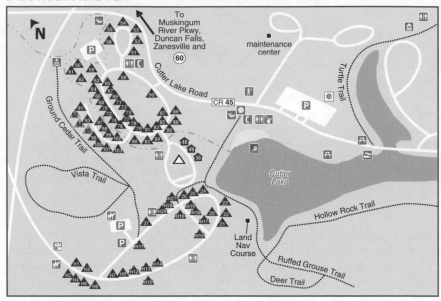

GETTING THERE

From I-70, take Exit 155 in Zanesville and follow OH 60 south 9.5 miles through Duncan Falls. Turn left on Cutler Lake Road and follow it 5.5 miles to Blue Rock State Park.

GPS COORDINATES: N39° 49.045' W81° 50.871'

18

⛺ Burr Oak Cove Campground

Beauty ★★★ Privacy ★★★ Spaciousness ★★★ Quiet ★★★★ Security ★★ Cleanliness ★★

This is a highlight of camping in the Wayne National Forest.

Wayne National Forest is comprised of three sections, all in southeastern Ohio and covering nearly 250,000 acres. Gracing a hillside of the northwestern section of the Wayne is Burr Oak Cove Campground. With its incredible beauty and many recreational opportunities, the forest is a great representative of the national forest system. The nearest town with an abundance of supplies and major retailers is Athens, a 20-mile drive south of the campground. The region is not exactly remote, but it is far enough away from the hustle and bustle of the human race to feel peaceful.

Burr Oak Cove Campground is only 1 mile from the entrance to Burr Oak State Park's campground, found by continuing on Burr Oak Road. The paved campground road quickly leads you to a self-service pay station. Campers have 30 minutes to return to the station and make the correct payment after selecting their site. The tall trees create a canopy over most of the campground, which provides cooler camping in the summer months and an impressive leaf-changing display in autumn. The 19 sites are divided along each side of the campground road that leads downhill after passing the pay station. Following the road downhill, the sites on the right side of the road have a brushy backdrop, while the sites on the left have a wooded ravine behind them. The sites on the right have ample room for an extra tent or a large cabin tent.

Burr Oak Cove Campground sits high on a wooded ridge above Burr Oak Lake.

KEY INFORMATION

LOCATION: Glouster

CONTACT: Operated by Wayne National
Forest, Athens Ranger District:
740-753-0101, fs.usda.gov/wayne

OPEN: Mid-April–mid-December

SITES: 19

EACH SITE HAS: Picnic table, fire ring

WHEELCHAIR ACCESS: Site 2 and updated
pit toilet are ADA-accessible.

ASSIGNMENT: First come, first served

REGISTRATION: At self-service pay station
at campground entrance

AMENITIES: Pit toilets, drinking water

PARKING: At each site

FEE: $15/night; once water is turned off
for winter, $10/night

ELEVATION: 875 feet

RESTRICTIONS

PETS: On leash and must clean up after

QUIET HOURS: 10 p.m.–6 a.m.

FIRES: In fire ring

ALCOHOL: Possession of alcohol is prohibited
in the Wayne National Forest per Ohio's
Open Container Law.

VEHICLES: Paved pad for 1

OTHER: Gathering deadwood from ground
for firewood is permitted; no holding sites
for guests arriving later; operation of ATVs
in campground prohibited; discharging firearms or fireworks prohibited; limited
supplies in Glouster

During spring and summer, various species of songbirds flittering about emit pleasant audio from early morning to well into the evening. The campground remains quiet enough for the birds' performances to be heard without interruption, even if a common flicker is pecking for a meal in a nearby tree as an addition to the show. A wide cul-de-sac at the bottom of the hill is surrounded with well-spaced sites.

Going back up the campground road, site 8 is on the right. It has a tight parking space, but the focal point of the site is 20 yards from the road, underneath the limbs of towering pines. A wildflower-covered ravine edge skirts two edges of the site. This spot catches a nice breeze yet is out of the primary wind from the southwest. Across the campground road from the pay station is site 2, an ADA-accessible site with a paved walkway leading to an updated pit toilet. The site is level, and the parking space is wide to accommodate a vehicle with a wheelchair lift.

Two major hiking trails—the North Country Trail and the Buckeye Trail—pass nearby, so it's common to meet thru-hikers at the campground. A connecting trail leads from the campground to the Lake View Trail, which winds from the dam to the marina of Burr Oak Lake. Nearby, several additional hiking trails lead hikers throughout Burr Oak State Park. Paddlers will find striking lake views at 644-acre Burr Oak Lake. From Burr Oak Cove Campground, follow Burr Oak Road to County Road 63 and turn right to find the marina and dock 4. This section of Wayne National Forest has well-paved roads that put road-touring enthusiasts in position for picturesque views of the lake and surrounding forest.

Burr Oak Cove Campground

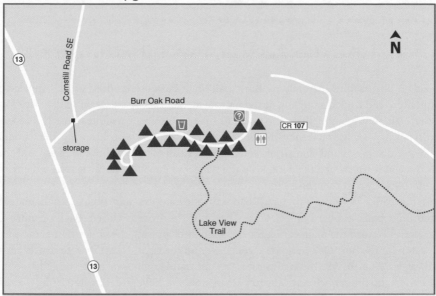

GETTING THERE

From Glouster, take OH 13 north 4.5 miles to Burr Oak Road/CR 107 and turn right. Follow Burr Oak Road 0.4 mile to the campground entrance on the right.

GPS COORDINATES: N39° 33.071' W82° 03.417'

19

⚠️Burr Oak State Park

Beauty ★★★ Privacy ★★★ Spaciousness ★★ Quiet ★★ Security ★★★ Cleanliness ★★★

This state park offers a touch of wilderness, with plenty of trails to explore it all.

The ridges and ravines surrounding Burr Oak State Park are foothills of the Appalachian Mountains. And a good sampling of the natural attractions of the Appalachians are found at Burr Oak. Spring and fall are the times to hike the trails or paddle across the 664-acre lake. In fall, especially, you'll enjoy the glowing foliage displays here. In spring, the woodland wildflower displays found along trails and roadsides call for shutterbugs to pause and shoot away. As you drive around the park, keep the windows down to allow the forested environment to please your other senses too.

At the camp store on Burr Oak Road, current camping and trail-use information is posted on a bulletin board on the store's porch if the store is closed. Back on Burr Oak Road, travel toward the main campground; soon after passing the equestrian camp on the left, watch for the Burr Oak water reservoir tower on the right. Near the water tower service driveway are sites 91–99. These campsites are not visible right away; you can only see them after driving up the service driveway to a small stone parking area. Situated along the ridge, these nine sites are the most secluded tent sites in the park. They require a short walk to

Multiple trails crisscross Burr Oak State Park.

KEY INFORMATION

LOCATION: 10220 Burr Oak Lodge Road Glouster, Ohio 45732

CONTACT: 740-767-3570, parks.ohiodnr.gov/burroak

OPEN: Year-round, including showers and water; other facilities limited in winter

SITES: 106 nonelectric, 17 electric

EACH SITE HAS: Picnic table, fire ring

WHEELCHAIR ACCESS: No specific ADA-accessible sites

ASSIGNMENT: Walk-in sites first come, first served; others may be reserved at 866-644-6727 or ohiostateparks.reserveamerica.com

REGISTRATION: At camp store; self-registration station on front of camp store

AMENITIES: Camp store, showers, flush toilets, laundry, playground, sports courts, boat ramp, boat rentals, disc-golf course, nature center

PARKING: At each site except for sites 91–96, which have a designated parking area

FEE: $26 electric, $22 nonelectric; $20 dock sites; $3 less November 1–March 31

ELEVATION: 896 feet

RESTRICTIONS

PETS: On leash only

QUIET HOURS: 10 p.m.–7 a.m.

FIRES: In fire ring

ALCOHOL: Prohibited in public areas in every state park but may be consumed within the confines of a rented cabin, cabin site, lodge room, or campsite

VEHICLES: 2/site

OTHER: Gathering firewood prohibited; 14-day stay limit

reach (approximately 60 feet to the first site), but the effort is well worth the privacy you gain away from the road. The slightly sloping sites are spread out on a finger ridge covered with a mix of hardwood trees and flank both sides of the trail leading through this section. The blue-blazed trail is a portion of a designated park trail that is often used by backpackers traveling through the park. There are no toilets here—you must drive 0.6 mile farther down Burr Oak Road to the main campground bathhouse or go back to the equestrian camp.

The main campground is located on a peninsula. Burr Oak Road ends at a cul-de-sac surrounded by sites 12–29. Ten of those sites overlook the lake, but they don't allow much space for large tents or direct access to the lake. The drop-off from sites 18–24 to the lake's edge is separated by safety netting to keep young campers from falling over the ledge. Sites 1–11 and 30–60 are suited for RVs and situated a bit close together. Sites 65–81 are tent-only and skirt a ridge edge—all 16 are situated on a shelf cut into a hillside. At a few of these sites, the steep slope from the parking space to the site makes it tough to maneuver from your vehicle and set up your camp. Site 67 is the best of these sites, as it provides the largest level area for a tent and a drinking-water spigot right next to it. Several boat docks are placed around the sprawling lake, and two have campsites—docks 2 and 3. Dock 2 has 11 sites, and dock 3 has 8 primitive sites.

The rugged geography of the park attracts many hikers and backpackers looking for challenging trails. Twenty-eight miles of the park's hiking trails include a stint on the state's Buckeye Trail and North Country Trail. The 14.7-mile Wildcat Hollow Backpack Trail is a star attraction and offers enough adventure for two days of trail time. Its trailhead is located on Burr Oak Lodge Road, off OH 78, which turns east off OH 13 just north of Glouster. The 1-mile Campground Trail runs from the equestrian camp to the main campground and mostly overlooks the lake.

Burr Oak State Park

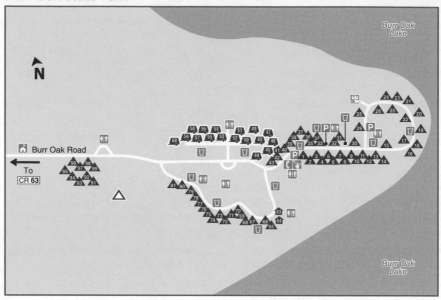

GETTING THERE

From Glouster, take OH 13 north 4.5 miles to Burr Oak Road/CR 107 and turn right. Follow Burr Oak Road 1.5 miles to the first campsites on the right. Continue on Burr Oak Road 0.3 mile to reach the main campground area.

GPS COORDINATES: N39° 32.572' W82° 02.391'

20

⚠ Forked Run State Park

Beauty ★★★ Privacy ★★ Spaciousness ★★ Quiet ★★ Security ★★★ Cleanliness ★★★

This rugged forest country overlooks the Ohio River.

Forked Run State Park touches the bank of the Ohio River and stretches up and into the rugged hills that were untouched by the last glaciers. The Forked Run region offers access to both land- and waterscapes. A public boat ramp on the Ohio River is only 0.8 mile west of the state park entrance on OH 124. Hiking trails, with several overlooks of the Ohio River to the south and forested, jagged hills to the north, meander around the state park.

Just as folks did a century or more ago—camped on a ridgetop high above the Ohio River—today's campers absorb the blend of senses-filling elements from the grand river and dense forest covering the crest. The campground consists of five sections set on top of three sharp hills. Area One, with sites 1–52, is on the shortest of the three mini-mountains and attracts RVers because of its proximity to amenities. A heated shower house sits in the center of Area One, with the amphitheater, playground, and rental cabins located along the road in Area One. To reach this area, take the first left after passing the campground office.

Forked Run Lake is a great place to cool off after a day of hiking.

Photo by Ohio Department of Natural Resources

KEY INFORMATION

LOCATION: 63300 OH 124
Reedsville, Ohio 45772-0127

CONTACT: 740-378-6206,
parks.ohiodnr.gov/forkedrun

OPEN: Year-round; in winter Area 1 sites are
open and water is available at the office.

SITES: 64 nonelectric, 81 electric

EACH SITE HAS: Picnic table, fire ring

WHEELCHAIR ACCESS: No specific
ADA-accessible sites

ASSIGNMENT: Walk-in sites first come, first
served; others may be reserved at 866-644-
6727 or ohiostateparks.reserveamerica.com

REGISTRATION: Self-registration station
at campground office, if campground
office closed

AMENITIES: Showers, vault toilets, laundry,
camp store, sports courts, playground,
swimming beach, boat rentals, disc-golf
course, nature programs in season

PARKING: At each site

FEE: $22 nonelectric, $30 electric;
deduct $3 in winter

ELEVATION: 649 feet

RESTRICTIONS

PETS: On leash only

QUIET HOURS: 10 p.m.–7 a.m.

FIRES: In fire ring, which must not be moved

ALCOHOL: Prohibited in public areas in every
state park but may be consumed within the
confines of a rented cabin, cabin site, lodge
room, or campsite

VEHICLES: 2/site

OTHER: Gathering firewood prohibited;
maximum 6 people/site

To find Area Two (sites 53–76), get back on the main campground road, take the next left, and ascend the second hill. Area Two's 23 sites offer electricity but still have a primitive feel. They are spread apart enough to gain a bit of privacy, and during the week, you may hardly see another person in this section. Site 67 sits at the top of this hill, at the outer edge of the cul-de-sac, and faces west. During autumn, site 67 puts leaf peepers in a front-row seat to enjoy a fall sunset over the Ohio River.

On around the main campground road from Area Two is a shower house at the cross-roads. Turn left to access Area Three, with sites 77–122. The sites are sprinkled along both sides of a snaking 0.7-mile incline to the highest peak—200 feet in elevation gain from the park entrance—before reaching a small loop. Halfway up the road on the left are sites 118 and 119. Set on a shelf cut along the ridge's back, both are pleasant spots to tent camp and feature views to the west, across a ravine and to a neighboring hilltop. At the top in the loop, site 100 sits next to a water spigot and faces the west for sunsets and stargazing. Near site 100 are two trailheads. The first is for the 2.6-mile Lakeview Trail. True to its name, this trail delivers a rigorous trek down the ridge within view of the lake. It continues around the side of the hill and arrives at the sandy swimming beach before turning and traversing the hill toward campground Area Three. The second trail, the 0.75-mile Riverview Trail, leads to a scenic overlook of the Ohio River coursing below.

Back at the intersection of campground roads, small Area Four (sites 123–130) sits on the left. This nonelectric section is too tight for anything more than a four-person dome tent. The parking spaces are at the road's edge, and campers must take a few steps down a slope to a small landing at wood's edge to reach the sites.

Return to the campground road, turn left, and follow it to Area Five (sites 131–151). This is the closet area to 120-acre Forked Run Lake, which has respectable crappie fishing.

It's tough to fish from the shore, as the steep hills plunge straight into the lake without any level bank to fish from. Since this park is well off the beaten path, the lake receives few boaters, so a kayak fishing excursion is in order here. Area Five's 20 sites are spotted along a sparsely shaded ridge. Most of the sites are well spaced and can accommodate a large tent, so they're perfect for families. Joining the state park is the 2,859-acre Shade River State Forest to the north. A short drive through the state forest via township roads reveals current forest-management practices in action.

Forked Run State Park

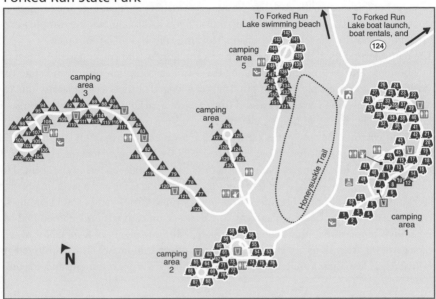

GETTING THERE

From Pomeroy, follow OH 7 northeast 6 miles to Chester. Take OH 248 east 9 miles to OH 124. Turn left and travel east 1.8 miles to the park entrance on the left.

GPS COORDINATES: N39° 05.503' W81° 46.335'

21

⛺ Hocking Hills State Park:
FAMILY HIKE-IN AREA

Beauty ★★★ Privacy ★★★ Spaciousness ★★★ Quiet ★★★ Security ★★ Cleanliness ★★

Caves, gorges, and waterfalls are all here at Ohio's premier hiking destination.

The mature deciduous trees of Hocking Hills perform one of the best autumn leaf color changes in the state. For this reason, the park has thousands of visitors in fall at both the campgrounds and roaming the park's roadways and hiking trails. If you had to choose one camping experience from this book for the fall foliage season, Hocking Hills should be your pick.

The natural wonders of this area are the caves and gorges, and you can easily access them by the abundant and well-maintained hiking trails and surrounding county and state roads. The park's caves are accessible even for physically challenged outdoors enthusiasts. One of the most popular caves, Ash Cave, is accessed from a paved parking area with restrooms, via a level, paved walking trail. Old Man's Cave, the most-visited cave of the park, is near the main campground entrance. Several parks are within a few minutes' drive of Old Man's Cave. For rock climbers, a designated area on Big Pine Road, off OH 374 in the Hocking Hills State Forest, offers 100-foot cliffs, chimneys, and overhangs to get a hands-on feel of the scenic Hocking Hills. For hikers, a newly opened trail leads to Whispering Cave and a swinging bridge.

Hocking Hills State Park sports one of the most popular family campgrounds in the state, which means it's buzzing on a regular basis. The park's main campground, named Old Man's Cave Family Campground, holds 156 electric sites that draw plenty of RVers. Not to worry, my tent-camping friends, as a nearby campground offers some relief. The primitive Family Hike-In Area is less than a mile away from the primary campground entrance. From the

Geology is the highlight at Hocking Hills State Park.

KEY INFORMATION

LOCATION: 19852 OH 664
Logan, Ohio 43138-9537

CONTACT: 740-385-6842,
parks.ohiodnr.gov/hockinghills

OPEN: Year-round; limited facilities Nov–Mar.

SITES: 33 nonelectric

EACH SITE HAS: Fire ring

WHEELCHAIR ACCESS: None at Family
Hike-In Area, but ADA-accessible sites and
restrooms available at the main campground
and office

ASSIGNMENT: Walk-in sites first come, first
served; others may be reserved at 866-644-
6727 or ohiostateparks.reserveamerica.com

REGISTRATION: At campground office at
main entrance on OH 664

AMENITIES: Family Hike-In Area: pit toilets,
potable water; main campground: showers,
flush toilets, laundry, camp store,
swimming pool

PARKING: In gravel parking area

FEE: $24 Apr.–Oct.; $21 Nov.–Mar.

ELEVATION: 1,020 feet

RESTRICTIONS

PETS: On leash only

QUIET HOURS: 10 p.m.–7 a.m.

FIRES: In fire ring

ALCOHOL: Prohibited in public areas in every
state park but may be consumed within the
confines of a rented cabin, cabin site, lodge
room, or campsite

VEHICLES: No vehicles permitted in Family
Hike-In Area; they must remain in parking
area at maintenance shop.

OTHER: Gathering firewood prohibited;
maximum 6 people/site

main office on OH 664, where you must register and pay for all campsites, travel north 0.5 mile to OH 374 and turn right. The next left leads to the hike-in campground parking area.

The parking area is adjacent to the park's maintenance shop, and a water spigot is available for campers between the parking area and the shop. Campers can access 33 tent sites on foot only. The campground lane extends over a half mile into the forest, rolling and alternating left and right only slightly; it's a moderate walk at best to reach even the most remote site. All sites are situated along the road, some only a step away from the road's edge and others a dozen or so yards to the left or right of it. The distance from the parking area to the first site is only 20 yards, but to reach the last site at the end of the road, a 0.6-mile hike is required. The road is stone, so no matter the weather, it's an easy walk. Watch out for the occasional mountain biker, though, as the 2-mile Purple Trail uses the campground road as a leg of its course.

Sites 1–5 are first come, first served, but the other 28 sites can be reserved. Pit toilets are located near the first site, just shy of halfway, and a few sites from the road's end. Site 6 is nearly hidden from the road thanks to a 20-yard path, but it does get some road noise from OH 374 through the forest. Site 8 is down a slope and more quiet, as OH 374 turns away from the campground slightly. Site 9 sits on a mound off to the right, nearly hidden if you aren't gazing up at the crown of a mix of oaks and hickories. Down the road 30 yards and to the left is site 29, which drops down a slant and curves out of site behind some young trees and heavy brush.

Near the halfway point is site 10, a wide site with ample space for a parent tent and a kiddie tent. This site is only a step off the road, so expect some "hellos." A narrow path lined with trees leads to site 28. Hardwood smoke from a campfire at site 28 will hang around the site because it's on the sheltered side of the road. Sites 12 and 28 are neighbors, with the road separating them. These sites work well for sociable campers and ones who don't mind the sounds of footsteps and bike tires passing nearby. Site 22 sits at the end of the road and 30 yards from the next to last site. It's wide, level, and the most private site. That is the reward for hauling all of your gear and accepting the fact that if you left something in the car, it would take a 1-mile-plus trek to get it and return. The difference in the highest and lowest elevation of the campground road is 40 feet. The road is four yards wide at its narrowest point, but it is nearly twice that for the most part.

About 0.5 mile south on OH 374 is a small parking area on the right. Leave the car and follow the 0.5-mile hiking trail to remote, 17-acre Rose Lake. The lake is stocked with rainbow trout annually, and a wide dam and a few points along the wooded shoreline offer a few casting spots. In spring, also keep a keen eye along the trail for some edible morel mushrooms that have just popped from the deciduous leaf clutter on the forest floor. Back at the new Old Man's Cave visitor center, displays and interpretive programs are regularly offered.

Hocking Hills State Park: Family Hike-In Area

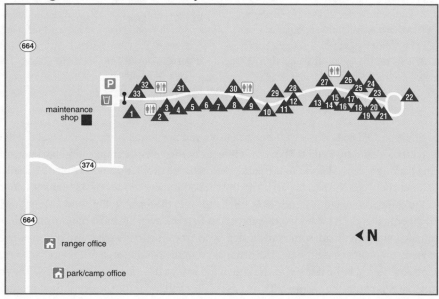

GETTING THERE

From Logan, travel south on OH 664 for 9.8 miles to OH 374 and turn left. Follow OH 374 for 0.3 mile to the park service lane and turn left. The Family Hike-In Area parking lot is straight ahead.

GPS COORDINATES: N39° 26.164' W82° 31.511'

22

⚑ Jesse Owens State Park

Beauty ★★★ Privacy ★★★ Spaciousness ★★★ Quiet ★★★★ Security ★★ Cleanliness ★★★

Ohio's newest state park offers tent campers two primitive campgrounds.

In 2018, the Ohio Department of Natural Resources purchased 5,735 acres of the American Electric Power Recreation Land in southeastern Ohio. Of that land purchase, 4,858 acres were designated as a wildlife area. The remaining 877 acres were designated as a state park, including two campgrounds—Campground C (Sand Hollow) and Campground G (Maple Grove). The new state lands were named Jesse Owens State Park and Wildlife Area. Currently, other than an application of stone coating to the camp roads, painted pit toilets, and signage, the campgrounds remain a primitive option for tenting as they were under the AEP Recreation Land title. The state has plans for some improvements, such as a water supply and improved restrooms, but there have been no confirmations as to when those will take place.

The larger of the two Jesse Owens State Park campgrounds, Campground C (Sand Hollow), rests at the northern border of the park. It stretches along the east side of a typical long and narrow reclaimed mining lake. The campground is popular, but with 45 sites spread out over 2.3 miles, it never feels crowded. Beginning at the entrance, the first mile skirts the lake's edge. The first five sites have direct access to the lake, which makes them tough to get unless you arrive before the weekend begins. As you travel north on the gravel road, sites

Popular Sand Hollow Campground has plenty of space for everyone.

KEY INFORMATION

LOCATION: 9290 OH 284
McConnelsville, OH 43756

CONTACT: Salt Fork State Park handles calls
for this park at 740-439-3521,
parksohiodnr.gov/jesseowens

OPEN: April–December

SITES: 45 at Sand Hollow, 11 at Maple Grove

EACH SITE HAS: Fire ring, picnic table

WHEELCHAIR ACCESS: None

ASSIGNMENT: First come, first served only

REGISTRATION: Self-registration at campground entrance

AMENITIES: Pit toilets, hand pump with
potable water

PARKING: At each site

FEE: Free

ELEVATION: 870 feet

RESTRICTIONS

PETS: On leash only

QUIET HOURS: 10 p.m.–7 a.m.

FIRES: In fire ring, which must not be moved

ALCOHOL: Prohibited in public areas in every
state park but may be consumed within the
confines of a rented cabin, cabin site, lodge
room, or campsite

VEHICLES: 2/site

OTHER: Gathering firewood prohibited;
maximum 6 people/site

on both sides get a bit dusty in the summer. The sites on the left have trails leading down a steep bank to the lake. The number of sites tapers off the farther north you travel on the gravel road. A T in the road marks the end of the campground. Turn around and proceed back to Campground C's entrance.

To visit Campground G (Maple Grove), return to OH 284, turn left, and drive 2 miles south to the entrance on the left. Campground G is situated on top of a wooded knoll. With only 11 sites, it's mostly quiet except for the road noise that is nearby and within sight.

A must-see while in the region is only 0.7 mile south of Campground G. Follow OH 284 south until it meets OH 78 and turn right. In 0.3 mile on the right is Miner's Memorial Park, where an important piece of gear is on display. The giant rusty bucket of the huge dragline named Big Muskie is the only remaining remnant of the massive machine that extracted coal from southeastern Ohio's surface beginning in 1969. It had a big hand in shaping the lands under and surrounding Jesse Owens State Park and Wildlife Area. The dragline's bucket weighs 460,000 pounds empty, and its volume equals a 12-car garage. An extensive informational display completes a visit to the park.

Jesse Owens State Park

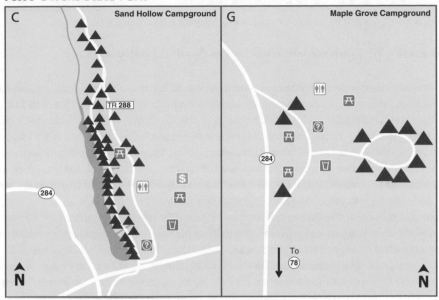

GETTING THERE

From Cumberland, to reach Campground C (Sand Hollow), follow OH 340 south 5 miles to Zeno. Turn left on OH 284 and continue south another 5 miles to Horse Run Road and turn left. Watch for park signage. Drive east on the gravel road 0.3 mile to the Campground C entrance on the left.

GPS COORDINATES
Campground C (Sand Hollow): N39° 44.037' W81° 43.864'
Campground G (Maple Grove): N39° 42.367' W81° 43.527'

23

⛺ Lake Alma State Park

Beauty ★★ Privacy ★★ Spaciousness ★★ Quiet ★★ Security ★★★ Cleanliness ★★★

This pleasing little park and lake are set in the Appalachian Highlands.

What was created to be a private amusement park during the early 1900s is now a naturally entertaining destination surrounding 60-acre Lake Alma, which includes an island in the middle for exploring. Lake Alma State Park is not a big park, but what it lacks in size it gains in quality. This lake is at its best for paddling and photography in spring and fall. Its aquatic diversity decorating the shoreline will keep shutterbugs busy for hours and paddlers entertained for a day or two. The lake and park are circled by a one-way park road, and one side is designated for walkers and bikers. Be sure to make a loop around the road and see what this little park has to offer before settling into your campsite for the night.

Spread out along the valley floor formed by two hills overlooking the eastern shore of Lake Alma is the primary campground. A small but pleasant camp office greets visitors with information on current events and a few supplies. Posted on exterior bulletin boards at the office are a series of photos of the park in action beginning nearly a century ago. Approximately 100 feet south of the office, on the left, is the entrance to the campsites. The first string of eight sites on the left is often filled with lengthy RVs, and the sites across the road from those offer little space for pitching a tent. As you drive farther up the narrow valley, the sites get more appealing.

Lake Alma is the perfect spot for a picnic.

KEY INFORMATION

LOCATION: 422 Lake Alma Road
Wellston, Ohio 45692

CONTACT: 740-384-4474,
parks.ohiodnr.gov/lakealma

OPEN: Year-round; limited facilities in winter,
but water still available

SITES: 10 nonelectric, 67 electric

EACH SITE HAS: Picnic table, fire ring

WHEELCHAIR ACCESS: ADA-accessible
shower house and restroom

ASSIGNMENT: Walk-in sites first come, first
served; others may be reserved at 866-644-
6727 or ohiostateparks.reserveamerica.com

REGISTRATION: At campground office; self-
registration station at office, if office closed

AMENITIES: Flush toilets, shower house,
water fountains, camp store, sports courts,
playground, swimming beach, boat rentals,
nature center

PARKING: At each site

FEE: $22 nonelectric, $26 electric;
deduct $3 in winter

ELEVATION: 687 feet

RESTRICTIONS

PETS: On leash only

QUIET HOURS: 10 p.m.–7 a.m.

FIRES: In fire ring, which must not be moved

ALCOHOL: Prohibited in public areas in every
state park but may be consumed within the
confines of a rented cabin, cabin site, lodge
room, or campsite

VEHICLES: 2/site

OTHER: Gathering firewood prohibited;
maximum 6 people/site

The next small group of sites on the right have more space for a tent spread. Sites 13 and 14 are the picks of the litter, as they offer the most room and a fire ring closer to the rear of the site, away from the campground road. As you pass site 17 on the right, turn right, and sites 20–28 will be visible lining one side of the paved road leading deep into a branch of the valley. These sites have a deep drainage ditch at their rear but provide ample room for setting up camp. Across the road from this row of sites is a steep, wooded hillside, from which you might see wild critters as they scamper about the cool bottom. At the end of the row, and sitting alone at the outer edge of the cul-de-sac, is site 28. To the left of site 28 is space for a minimal camp set-up. To the right of the site is a wider grassy area. At the rear of that grassy area is a wooden footbridge that accesses the 0.75-mile Sassafras Trail, which climbs north over the southern forested hill and arrives near the campground entrance.

Travel back to the road intersection near site 17 and stay to the right. At that intersection is a shower house, which is an easy 100-foot walk from site 28. The campground continues up the ravine as it narrows, with sites 36–40 at the end of the dead-end road. These five sites have trees guarding the corners of the parking spaces, which makes backing an RV into the sites a challenge. With RVs being scared away from this area, tent campers should have the quiet end all to themselves. Behind the sites is a small stream for the kids to explore. During heavy rain, the stream will fill suddenly because of the steepness of the surrounding, quickly draining hills. But the creekbanks are high enough to keep most rains contained and out of the campsites. Site 36 is the last site on the road, and because there is no place to turn around except for the parking space of site 36, sightseeing vehicles may be unwelcome guests from time to time.

Ten primitive sites are set along Little Raccoon Creek on the opposite side of the lake. Sites 68–77 are on the west side of OH 349, near the park entrance. Not all of the sites are marked, but a picnic table and fire ring reveal the site's location. In the same area are a shelter house and a basketball court, which attract families, so privacy and complete solitude are not likely at these 10 primitive sites. Water is available at the shelter house via a drinking fountain, and a pit toilet sits near the parking area.

Five miles to the northwest of the state park is the Leo Petroglyph State Memorial, preserved and protected by the Ohio Historical Society and containing 37 drawings of animals and humans. The drawings, mysterious in their meanings, were created by the Fort Ancient Indians more than 500 years ago. The small park includes an observation deck and a walking trail through the sandstone gorge, which provided protection to the Indians. To find the memorial and its small parking lot, leave Lake Alma State Park and go south to Wellston. Travel northwest on OH 327 for 6.3 miles to County Road 30 and turn left. Follow CR 30 for 2.2 miles to CR 29 and turn left. Travel 0.6 miles to Township Road 224 and turn right. Follow TR 224 for 0.5 mile to the parking lot on the left.

Lake Alma State Park

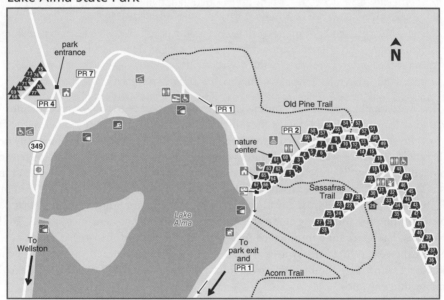

GETTING THERE

From Wellston, go north on OH 93 for 0.7 mile to OH 349. Turn right and travel 1.5 miles to the park entrance on the right. Follow the park road 0.5 mile to the campground entrance on the left.

GPS COORDINATES: N39° 08.786' W82° 30.589'

24

⛺ Lake Hope State Park

Beauty ★★ Privacy ★★★ Spaciousness ★★★ Quiet ★★★ Security ★★★★ Cleanliness ★★★

Expect adventurous tent camping at Lake Hope State Park.

The glacial meltwaters that carved their way through southeastern Ohio left behind a rugged landscape. Thousands of years later, those ravines and their accompanying ridges are now covered with forests and interspersed meadows offering nature lovers a paradise to explore. When visiting Lake Hope State Park, pack a pair of sturdy hiking boots and/or a trusty mountain bike because the park has more than 23 miles of trails—some multiuse and some dedicated to one user type.

While driving to and through this state park, it quickly becomes evident that you are somewhere special. Surrounded by the Zaleski State Forest, the park offers nearly limitless adventure: rock climbing, extreme hiking, serious mountain biking, kayaking, and horseback riding on what may be the most beautiful equine trail in the state. A wildflower guidebook will also be useful while visiting Zaleski, as the forest is home to numerous species, such as blue-eyed Mary and wild geranium to name a few. The 120-acre Lake Hope is impressive in its own right and fills the senses, whether you're skimming across its surface in a kayak or a canoe or simply siting at its edge and dangling a toe into the crystal clear water.

The pleasant campground sees many repeat campers for several reasons, but the primary ones are the abundance of outdoor pursuits available nearby and the gorgeous scenery

Anglers have great luck at Lake Hope.

KEY INFORMATION

LOCATION: 27331 OH 278
McArthur, Ohio 45651

CONTACT: 740-596-4938,
parks.ohiodnr.gov/lakehope

OPEN: Year-round; limited facilities in winter,
including heated shower house

SITES: 141 nonelectric, 46 electric

EACH SITE HAS: Picnic table, fire ring

WHEELCHAIR ACCESS: ADA-accessible
shower house

ASSIGNMENT: Walk-in sites first come, first
served; others may be reserved at 866-644-
6727 or ohiostateparks.reserveamerica.com

REGISTRATION: At campground office; self-
registration station at office, if office closed

AMENITIES: Heated shower house and flush
toilets, laundry, pay phone, nature center,
playground, sports courts, boat ramp and
boat rentals at Lake Hope

PARKING: At each site

FEE: $22 nonelectric, $26 electric;
deduct $3 in winter

ELEVATION: 919 feet

RESTRICTIONS

PETS: On leash only

QUIET HOURS: 10 p.m.–7 a.m.

FIRES: In fire ring, which must not be moved

ALCOHOL: Prohibited in public areas in every
state park but may be consumed within the
confines of a rented cabin, cabin site, lodge
room, or campsite

VEHICLES: 2/site; additional parking available
but scattered

OTHER: Gathering firewood prohibited;
visitors must register at park office on
OH 278; major retailers in Nelsonville

that complements those activities. Campground sites are staged along a 2.5-mile-long ridge covered with a mix of deciduous and evergreen forest and with occasional views overlooking deep valleys and other ridgetops. After passing the active nature center and then the campground office, walk-in sites 1–25 and 177–189 are first come, first served and located on the right and left. As the ridge continues to rise as you travel, sites 29–32 require a short, steep walk downhill from their parking spaces. Those sites are perched on a ledge with limited views of the next ridge. During fall, these ridges seem to glow orange and bright red for miles because of the transforming leaves. The main shower house is located near sites 62–89 (a second shower house is located near the camp office). Those sites have electricity and are usually taken by RVs.

Leave the shower house area and continue on through a gate that is closed during winter months. After passing through the open gate, tent campers should feel more at home in sites 90–125, which grace the top of a smaller finger ridge. This section of the campground is shaded with large pines and gets a steady breeze, which can become testy during summer thunderstorms, so be sure those tent stakes are secure. With the wind whispering through the pine branches and the aroma of old and new pine needles, this section also feels and appears similar to a western mountain forest campground. Sites 100–108 are suited for smaller tents and campers with very little gear. Sites 109 and 114 are small group sites. The Habron Hollow Trail is accessible from site 114 and flows down the ridge for more than 1.5 miles to where another hiking trail, the White Oak Trail, comes in from the left. Follow this adjoining trail for a nice 0.25-mile trek to the camp office.

Two mountain bike trails split off the Habron Hollow Trail: the Red Oak Bike Trail leads back to the campground's main road, and the 7.2-mile Copperhead Bike Trail, which meets Cabin Ridge Road, just north of the park's cabin area.

A first-class nature center draws its share of folks of all ages to interact with naturalists and explore the many displays consistently available at the center. During July and August, a popular pastime at the nature center is feeding hummingbirds—by hand. Some interesting facts of the area's past include the iron furnaces that were a bustling industry. The Hope Furnace was used more than 100 years ago to process the iron ore taken from the region's sandstone. The iron was then used for items such as ammunition cannons for the Union Army during the Civil War. The charcoal fires that were kept 24 hours a day used large quantities of wood from the area, until the iron smelting ceased here around 1900. Today, the forests have been regenerated, and the Hope Furnace chimney and a portion of the foundation remain near the campground entrance.

Lake Hope State Park

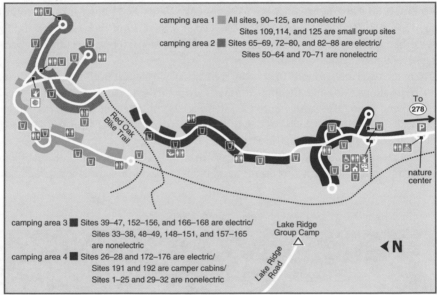

GETTING THERE

From US 33 in Nelsonville, take OH 278 south 13.5 miles to Furnace Ridge Road and turn right. Travel up the steep, winding road 0.5 mile to the campground office.

GPS COORDINATES: N39° 20.147' W82° 20.430'

⚕Lake Vesuvius Recreation Area

Beauty ★★★★ Privacy ★★★ Spaciousness ★★★ Quiet ★★★★ Security ★★★ Cleanliness ★★★

Lake Vesuvius is one of Ohio's premium tent-camping destinations.

Gazing out over the dense Wayne National Forest at the Lake Vesuvius Recreation Area today, one can hardly imagine the hills bare of trees as they were in the 1800s. This was because of the extensive timber harvesting necessary to fuel the iron-ore furnaces that were active in the region at that time. What is visible today is the result of years of hard work initiated by the Civilian Conservation Corps during the 1930s and the recreational opportunities created by the forest managers over the last several decades. More than 1,200 acres of big woods are here to explore, as is 143-acre Lake Vesuvius. Healthy hikers can hit the 8-mile Lakeshore Trail, which chases the lake's edge with views of rock outcrops and footbridge crossings for an up-close look at this part of the national forest. Start that trek at any of the several parking sites around the lake.

There are two campgrounds to choose from at Lake Vesuvius. Both have gone through major renovations. Although the improvements attract RVers, plenty of sites still appeal to tent campers. From OH 93, turn onto County Road 29, and the first road on the left leads to Oak Hill Campground, which has newly paved roads and site pads, updated shower and toilet facilities, and plenty of electric and water.

The other campground at Lake Vesuvius is Iron Ridge Campground, and that's where the tent campers go. To reach it, continue east on CR 29, pass below the lake's spillway and a

This iron furnace at Lake Vesuvius was built during the late 1800s.

KEY INFORMATION

LOCATION: Pedro

CONTACT: Operated by Wayne National Forest, Ironton Ranger District: 740-534-6500, fs.usda.gov/wayne

OPEN: April–October

SITES: Iron Ridge: 21 nonelectric, 20 electric; Oak Hill: 8 nonelectric, 32 electric

EACH SITE HAS: Picnic table, fire ring, tent pad

WHEELCHAIR ACCESS: 3 sites and the lakeside boardwalk are ADA-accessible.

ASSIGNMENT: Walk-in sites first come, first served; others may be reserved at 866-644-6727 or ohiostateparks.reserveamerica.com

REGISTRATION: Self-registration station at bulletin board; check for reserved sites posted on the bulletin board before setting up as a first-come, first-serve camper.

AMENITIES: Showers, flush toilets, pit toilets, water spigots, swimming beach

PARKING: At each site

FEE: $20 electric, $15 nonelectric; senior and access pass $12.50 electric, $7.50 nonelectric

ELEVATION: 600 feet

RESTRICTIONS

PETS: On leash and attended

QUIET HOURS: 10 p.m.–6 a.m.

FIRES: In fire ring

ALCOHOL: Possession of alcohol is prohibited in Wayne National Forest per Ohio's Open Container Law.

VEHICLES: 2/site

OTHER: No nails or damage to trees; maximum 8 people or immediate family per site

historic iron-ore furnace on the right, and take the next road on the left. This dead-end road snakes uphill to Iron Ridge and has sites on each side all the way to a small loop. The campground stretches over 0.5 mile. At the entrance to this ideal woodland camping experience, there's a self-registration station and bulletin board on the right. To the left is the first site, which is typically occupied by a campground host.

Uphill from site 8 on the left is a small parking area and pit toilet for several walk-in sites. These spots populate the top of a finger ridge facing south. Even with the heavy forest cover, expect some sun rays to penetrate and warm up camp. It's 40 yards from the parking area to the last walk-in site. Each site is staggered down the ridge to give plenty of privacy. Set up camp and enjoy the aroma, sights, and sounds of this healthy deciduous and evergreen forest.

Nearing the top of the ridge is another set of walk-in sites. These three sites differ from the first set of walk-in sites because they run parallel to the road and are less than 10 yards from the road's edge. From the small parking area, there are no sites until you reach the loop at the end of the road. Inside the loop are a pit toilet and a water spigot. As the loop turns and begins to descend, a site sits on the outside with the highest viewpoint from the ridge. Next to this site, you can pick up the Whiskey Run Trail, a 0.5-mile hiking trail that connects the campground to the lake and the Lakeshore Trail, 150 feet below the top of the ridge.

Lake Vesuvius is as picturesque as a big forest lake gets. It is accessible by everyone thanks to the 0.3-mile-long boardwalk that links the dam and spillway to the south to the boat dock at the northern tip of the lake's western branch. The boardwalk skirts the shoreline and includes several wide sections for anglers to cast a line without any interference. Beginning at the boat dock parking lot is the 0.75-mile Rock House Trail, an interpretive, paved trail that leads to a rock shelter and other geologic formations.

Lake Vesuvius Recreation Area

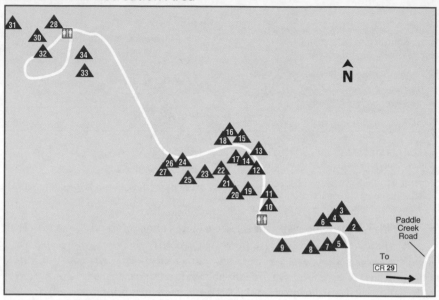

GETTING THERE

From Ironton, travel north on OH 93 for 6 miles to CR 29 on the right. Follow CR 29 for 0.8 mile to a park road on the left. Follow this forest road to Oak Hill Campground. Stay on CR 29 for another 1.2 miles and then take another road on the left to arrive at Iron Ridge Campground.

GPS COORDINATES: N38° 36.282' W82° 37.931'

26

⚠ Leith Run Recreation Area

Beauty ★★★ Privacy ★★★ Spaciousness ★★★ Quiet ★★★ Security ★★ Cleanliness ★★★★

You'll be mesmerized by the mighty but gentle Ohio River that flows near this campground.

Camping along the Ohio River is the perfect way to soak up some major river atmosphere. The campground at Leith Run is favored by a mix of camping enthusiasts, including tent campers, who have three sites dedicated to their method of camping. And the 18 sites that provide utilities rivaling a well-developed town are also spaced far enough apart to welcome a family of tent campers to drop in between the rigs. Sites 11 and 19 sit on the mowed and well-maintained bank of the Ohio River, and since your focus will be on the river, you likely won't care what your neighbors are sleeping in. During my stay there, I soon realized the place was as quiet, relaxed, and orderly as I've ever seen in a campground that allows RVs. Each site is equipped with a first-class fire ring/grill combo that begs to be used. There is something stirring about campfire smoke lingering along the banks of a grand river. Sitting in the center of the open woodland campground are relatively new, well-maintained shower houses.

You'll find the three tent sites at the east side of the property; all require a 30-yard walk to reach them. Popular site 21 sits on the Ohio River's edge. The riverbank beckons campers to drag out a comfortable chair and sit a spell. If it wasn't for the occasional string of barges

Leith Run Recreation Area lies in the heart of the Wayne National Forest.

LOCATION: 44400 OH 7
New Matamoras, Ohio 45767

CONTACT: Operated by Wayne National
Forest, Athens Ranger District, Marietta Unit:
740-373-9055, fs.usda.gov/wayne

OPEN: April 15–October 15

SITES: 3 nonelectric tent sites,
18 full-service sites

EACH SITE HAS: Picnic table, fire ring,
lantern post

WHEELCHAIR ACCESS: ADA-accessible sites,
shower house, and playground

ASSIGNMENT: Walk-in sites first come, first
served; others may be reserved at 866-644-
6727 or ohiostateparks.reserveamerica.com

REGISTRATION: Self-registration station at
bulletin board; check for reserved sites
posted on the bulletin board before setting
up as a first-come, first-serve camper.

AMENITIES: Showers, flush toilets,
playground, sports courts

PARKING: At each site, except tent-only sites
use a parking lot next to the shower house.

FEE: $20 full-service, $15 nonelectric;
$10 reservation fee

ELEVATION: 615 feet

RESTRICTIONS
PETS: On leash only

QUIET HOURS: 10 p.m.–6 a.m.

FIRES: In fire ring

ALCOHOL: Possession of alcohol is prohibited
in Wayne National Forest per Ohio's Open
Container Law.

VEHICLES: 2/site; overflow parking available
in lot

OTHER: Downed wood from the ground may
be gathered for firewood; maximum 8
people/site; 14-day stay limit

being pushed with a tugboat, it would be easy to believe at any moment a log raft with a straw-hat-wearing captain might come floating by.

Between the riverside sites of the campground's main section and site 21 are a raised, wooden observation deck and a picnic shelter. This area is considered a day-use area, so expect a few visitors to pass by your tent site until darkness falls. Bring a pair of binoculars to this point and whittle away some time surveying up and down the river. You will see critters visiting the riverbank to slurp a drink and maybe even get a close-up shot of a sternwheeler with tourists waving. Sites 20 and 22 are on the banks of Leith Run, the Ohio River tributary that gives the recreation area its name. A footpath leads from the heart of the campground to a fishing pier at the most extreme eastern point of the property and where the tributary enters the river. Upstream from that confluence and the tent sites is an old boat ramp that is no longer in use. Siltation has reduced the water depth there to only a couple of feet. However, canoeists and kayakers can still use the ramp as an entry point.

Leith Run Recreation Area is the perfect place to kick back and simply rest and relax. But if hiking is your forte, consider tackling the 4-mile Scenic River Trail, which is accessible from the campground. The trail crosses OH 7 (marked with signage) and ends near the German Cemetery on County Road 9. It's blazed with yellow and white diamonds to keep you on track, but only hard-core hikers should consider it. The path winds up and around steep ridges, with occasional vistas of the Ohio River, rock outcrops, and sizable trees as highlights. Even if you trek up only 1 mile before turning back toward the campground, it'll be worth the effort. Oh, and don't be surprised if a black bear scampers across the path in front of you, as this section of the Wayne National Forest has several bear sightings each year.

Leith Run Recreation Area

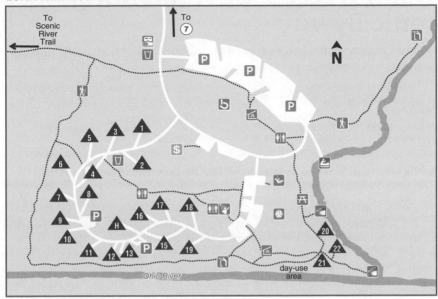

GETTING THERE

From I-77, take Exit 1 in Marietta and travel east on OH 7 for 20.4 miles to the campground entrance on the right.

GPS COORDINATES: N39° 26.986' W81° 08.784'

27

⛺ National Forest Covered Bridge Scenic Byway

LANE FARM CAMPGROUND: Beauty ★★ Privacy ★ Spaciousness ★★ Quiet ★ Security ★★ Cleanliness ★

HUNE BRIDGE CAMPGROUND: Beauty ★★ Privacy ★ Spaciousness ★★ Quiet ★★ Security ★★ Cleanliness ★

RING MILL CAMPGROUND: Beauty ★★ Privacy ★★ Spaciousness ★★★★ Quiet ★★★ Security ★ Cleanliness ★★

LAMPING HOMESTEAD RECREATION AREA: Beauty ★★★ Privacy ★★★ Spaciousness ★★★ Quiet ★★★★ Security ★ Cleanliness ★★★

Take this one beautiful byway to experience four national forest campgrounds.

The National Forest Covered Bridge Scenic Byway is a 44-mile tour through southeastern Ohio. The designated scenic stretch of winding and rolling OH 26 runs from Marietta to Woodsfield, cutting through a mix of agricultural and forest landscapes. The covered bridges from the horse-and-buggy days of the 1800s still stand proud and welcome the attention of admirers. This stretch of road also lies in a portion of the Wayne National Forest, which adds a touch of wild country to the trip. Wandering alongside the byway for many of the 44 miles is the Little Muskingum River. This pleasant little river sees paddlers nearly year-round. For the most part, the stream slowly finds its way to the Muskingum River that dumps into the Ohio River at Marietta. Situated along the Little Muskingum River and the byway are

Hills Covered Bridge is one of four covered bridges on the scenic byway.

KEY INFORMATION

LOCATION: Marietta

CONTACT: Operated by Wayne National Forest, Athens Ranger District, Marietta Unit: 740-373-9055, fs.usda.gov/wayne

OPEN: Year-round

SITES: Lane Farm, 4; Hune Bridge, 4; Ring Mill, 3; Lamping Homestead, 6

EACH SITE HAS: Picnic table, fire ring

WHEELCHAIR ACCESS: None

ASSIGNMENT: First come, first served

REGISTRATION: No registration

AMENITIES: Pit toilets

PARKING: At each site, except Lamping Homestead has parking area

FEE: $10/night

ELEVATION: Lane Farm, 612 feet; Hune Bridge, 637 feet; Ring Mill, 679 feet; Lamping Homestead, 734 feet

---

RESTRICTIONS

PETS: On leash only and must clean up after

QUIET HOURS: 10 p.m.–6 a.m.

FIRES: In fire ring

ALCOHOL: Possession of alcohol is prohibited in Wayne National Forest per Ohio's Open Container Law.

VEHICLES: Multiple allowed

OTHER: Gathering deadwood from ground for firewood is permitted; no holding sites for guests arriving later; operation of ATVs in campground is prohibited; discharging firearms or fireworks prohibited; 14-day stay limit; most supplies available in Marietta and Woodsfield

four small campgrounds, each with its own taste to satisfy campers with different camping appetites. Note that the campgrounds seem to get better in regard to tent camping, and the elements that make tenting such an exciting adventure, as you travel northeast on the byway.

Beginning in Marietta, travel 5 miles on OH 26 and you'll first reach Lane Farm Campground. These four sites perched on a high bank of the Little Muskingum receive more traffic than the others because of their proximity to town. This campground is just off OH 26, and the road noise is a constant presence. Canoeists and kayakers can launch near site 1 here. Sites 1 and 2 offer the best shade for summer camping, and likely the most space if friends are along for the river excursion. A unisex pit toilet is a short walk from the sites, but it's not too close to annoy the nose. The North Country Trail drops into camp from the opposite side of the river. During average water levels, you should be able to cross the river with caution, but hold your packs up high.

Driving northeast on OH 26 for 12 miles from Lane Farm Campground, you will see Hune Bridge on the right. Cross the bridge to find Hune Bridge Campground on the south side. Three sites are spaced well apart, with the last site on the river. At this point, the Little Muskingum River is wider with a broad strip of gravel riverbank. The easy access to the water is great for launching canoes and kayaks, as well as fishing. Look for two interpretive signs at Hune Bridge Campground. The first provides historical information about the bridge, and the other explains the importance of the oil and gas industry of today in the region. An oil-gathering tank, complete with lines slithering out of the forest and into the tank, is on display at the campground. A trailhead allows access to a 5-mile hiking trail that leads to the Rinard Covered Bridge to the northeast.

The next campground is not within eye or earshot of OH 26. From Hune Bridge, follow OH 26 northeast 14.5 miles to County Road 68 on the right. Drive 2.7 miles to Township Road 575 on the right, cross the bridge over the Little Muskingum River, and the Ring Mill

Campground lane is on the left. After entering the lane, you will see an old stone building on the right. An interpretive sign next to the road tells the story of the building's history as the home of the family that ran a mill on the site during the mid 1800s (it's listed on the National Register of Historic Places). Take a moment here and absorb what you read and see, then let your mind imagine what life was like at that place 150 years ago. Continue on down the lane to three campsites and a new shelter house. A pit toilet is located near the stone building. Site 3 is on the river, and sites 1 and 2 are back from the river but still neighbor site 3. Direct access to the river from site 3 is difficult, as the bank is steep, but a canoe access lane is adjacent to the site. The campground is mostly shaded except for the open canopy bordering the lane. Ring Mill may be the least visited of the four campgrounds. It's also a trailhead for the North Country Trail and the Buckeye Trail, Ohio's encompassing hiking trail.

Return to OH 26 and resume the tour for 2.9 miles to OH 537 on the left. Follow this road 1.6 miles up and around a tall ridge, which allows a great view of the valley you just came through, before descending the back side of the ridge to Clearfork Road on the left. Go 0.15 mile to the Lamping Homestead Recreation Area and its campground—one of Ohio's best tent-camping opportunities and relatively unknown, well, until now. Park your car in the gravel parking area and look toward the large pond beyond the mowed field. The six sites (and picnic shelter) are tucked under the towering pines on the pond's left edge—you have to walk approximately 60 yards from the parking area to the campsites. The field is level, which makes for easy walking if you have extra gear for a multiday trip. A pit toilet is located near the parking area, where you'll also find a bulletin board with information, including advice for keeping food stored to deter bear visits. Yes, bears. They exist in eastern Ohio. The sites are equally level and pleasantly situated so that each camper can wake and peek out the tent door and observe the misty pond. The 2-acre pond is not only pleasant to look at but also offers some decent fishing. It's stocked with bass, bluegill, and catfish, so pack a rod and reel. Even if all six sites are occupied, there's plenty of space for all campers to experience the remote, wild essence here. Two hiking trails loop out into the forest from the campground. One is 1.5 miles, and the other is a 3.5-mile trek with several views from the surrounding ridges. A cemetery for some of the Lamping family members rests on a hill above the campground. The Lampings settled on the property in the early 1800s, before sickness and hard living forced the remaining family members to move on. What exists on the site today is a retreat from today's trials and tribulations that cause grief for folks in town. Interesting how the past and present contradict each other sometimes in certain places.

GETTING THERE

From I-77, take Exit 1 in Marietta and go west on OH 7. Turn right onto Acme Street (first traffic light) and drive 0.6 mile to Greene Street (OH 26). Turn right and travel 5 miles to Lane Farm Campground on the right.

GPS COORDINATES
Lane Farm Campground: N39° 26.145' W81° 21.553'
Hune Bridge Campground: N39° 30.573' W81° 15.014'
Ring Mill Campground: N39° 36.445' W81° 7.320'
Lamping Homestead Recreation Area: N39° 37.823' W81° 11.423'

National Forest Covered Bridge Scenic Byway

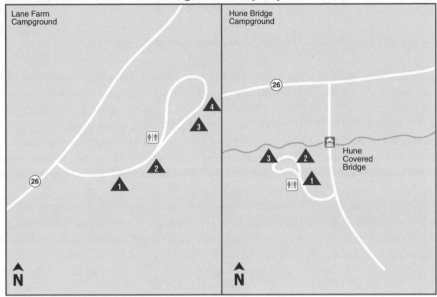

National Forest Covered Bridge Scenic Byway

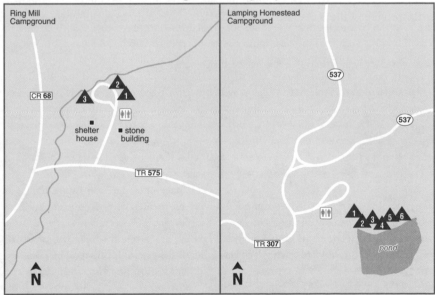

28

⛺Piedmont Lake

Beauty ★★★ Privacy ★ Spaciousness ★★ Quiet ★★ Security ★★★ Cleanliness ★★

The sense of a remote Canadian lake atmosphere overcomes visitors here.

The Muskingum Watershed Conservancy District (MWCD) manages more than 8,000 square miles and 14 lakes throughout eastern Ohio. Of those lakes, Piedmont Lake and its surroundings may be the most special of the group in regard to outdoor recreation with a dose of nostalgia. The MWCD was created to control flooding in the expansive watershed that feeds the Muskingum River. The big job of planning and constructing dams began in the early 1930s. Of course, the dams were created for flood control and water conservation, but they soon became playgrounds for outdoor adventurers. Piedmont became a favorite for many only a few years after completion.

Today, the atmosphere of a relaxed wilderness location still exists and is appreciated. The campground is frequented by anglers and those who captain the many pontoon boats moored at the marina. The short drive down a fairly steep grade from OH 800 to the marina and campground seems like a time portal, with a lake paradise greeting those who make the trip back in time. Once at the marina store, the campground is located just around the corner. There is only one road into the marina/campground area, which keeps traffic noise to a bare minimum. The campground rests in a cove, and when the wind comes out of the east, a cool lake breeze filters through the camp.

In 2010, interest from petroleum companies in oil and natural gas deposits beneath eastern Ohio brought a substantial amount of land lease money to landowners and managers sitting on top of those resources. The MWCD is one of those entities experiencing the

You can rent a variety of watercraft at the marina at Piedmont Lake.

KEY INFORMATION

LOCATION: 32281 Marina Road
Freeport, Ohio 43973

CONTACT: Operated by Muskingum Watershed Conservancy District: 740-658-1029, piedmontmarina.mwcd.org

OPEN: Year-round

SITES: 71 electric

EACH SITE HAS: Picnic table, fire ring

WHEELCHAIR ACCESS: Restrooms

ASSIGNMENT: Walk-in sites first come, first served; others may be reserved at 866-644-6727 or ohiostateparks.reserveamerica.com

REGISTRATION: At Piedmont Marina store; if closed, follow self-registration directions posted at store

AMENITIES: Supply store, showers, flush toilets and pit toilets, drinking water, playground, direct access to the lake, boat rentals

PARKING: At each site

FEE: $31.50

ELEVATION: 920 feet

RESTRICTIONS

PETS: On leash only in designated areas

QUIET HOURS: 11 p.m.–7 a.m.

FIRES: In fire ring

ALCOHOL: None publicly consumed or displayed

VEHICLES: 2/site

OTHER: 2 tents maximum/site; must be age 18 or over to register for campsite

financial gains, and it has developed a plan to invest in its parks by renovating infrastructure over the next couple of decades. As of 2020, campgrounds of the MWCD parks were seeing upgraded sites, camper facilities, and construction of additional camping opportunities. Although the MWCD parks are updating the campgrounds to accommodate the power demands of new, bigger RVs, tent campers still have a place at these parks. Actually, a couple of new primitive camps are in the current plans, so be sure to ask about future tent-camping sections when making reservations.

Although the campground is inhabited by several seasonal campers, a fair share of overnight sites remain open for tenters. The lakeside sites are taken by seasonals, but a walkway to the lake for all campers passes through those sites. A group of nine level sites surrounded by the looping campground road have the nearest access to the lake and are targeted by RVers. At the west end of this loop is the primary shower house. The best tent sites that offer the most solitude are found in the northwest edge of this compact campground. This string of sites is spaced nicely along the base of a forested hill with an abundance of hardwood trees standing guard throughout the sites. This campground in the cove is a pleasant place to rest after a day of boating around Piedmont Lake's 38 miles of gorgeous shoreline.

The North Country Trail, which shares the same path with the Buckeye Trail at many points around Ohio including this one, passes through Piedmont. This portion of the established hiking trail leads around the lower portion of three primary ridges that disappear into Piedmont Lake. The trail is maintained by volunteers of the Buckeye Trail Association. Be sure to bring your camera fully charged, as this 4.7-mile stretch of trail offers a multitude of photographic opportunities. At the 2.1-mile point from a rest area along OH 22, the lake's impressive length comes into view. If you go the full length of the Piedmont section, you will end up at Thin Lane, which connects to Marina Road. At the 4.5-mile point, the trail passes near the most western edge of the campground.

Piedmont Lake Campground

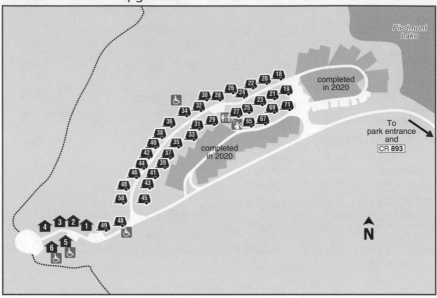

GETTING THERE

From I-77, northeast of Cambridge, take Exit 47 to US 22. Travel east 20.3 miles to OH 800, and then proceed south 0.6 mile to Marina Road/CR 893. Take Marina Road 1.1 miles to Piedmont Marina.

GPS COORDINATES: N40° 09.979' W81° 13.574'

29

⛺ Salt Fork State Park:
PRIMITIVE CAMPGROUND

Beauty ★★★ Privacy ★★★ Spaciousness ★★ Quiet ★★★★ Security ★★★★ Cleanliness ★★★

Discover quiet camping in Ohio's largest state park.

Salt Fork State Park is Ohio's largest state park. Not only does it earn this title because of its expansive spread, but also for the plethora of natural recreation available. The park's name was derived from a salt source utilized by American Indians. The region boasts several geographical highlights that attract visitors year-round. The forested ravines are believed by some to be the home of the Ohio Grassman—Ohio's version of Bigfoot. I'm not too sure about that, but the natural landscape does provide the perfect tent-camping environment.

This unglaciated countryside welcomes those who enjoy a multimile hike among sandstone boulders decorating forested hills, as well as those who prefer a day on the water with a rod and reel or making wakes with a paddle or outboard. An 18-hole golf course lies in the center of the park, and a minigolf course is at the beach. The variety of activities around the park is as diverse as the camping. A 200-plus-site modern campground provides amenity-rich camping, but for the tent camper, the park has just the place for a quiet night's sleep and a peaceful day of relaxation—an isolated primitive campground that's disconnected from the main campground.

Keep an eye out for Bigfoot at Salt Fork's primitive campground.

KEY INFORMATION

LOCATION: 14755 Cadiz Road
Lore City, Ohio 43755-9602

CONTACT: 740-432-1508 (seasonal camp office), 740-439-3521 (park office);
parks.ohiodnr.gov/saltfork

OPEN: Year-round; camp store is closed December–March, but one heated shower building is open in main campground

SITES: 24

EACH SITE HAS: Fire ring, shared picnic tables

WHEELCHAIR ACCESS: None

ASSIGNMENT: First come, first served

REGISTRATION: At main campground office; self-registration also at campground office

AMENITIES: Pit toilets, drinking water, dishwater disposal; all amenities at the main campground available for primitive campground occupants (showers, flush toilets, laundry, beach, boat launch)

PARKING: At designated parking areas (short walk to sites required)

FEE: $20

ELEVATION: 999 feet

RESTRICTIONS

PETS: On leash only

QUIET HOURS: 10 p.m.–7 a.m.

FIRES: In fire ring

ALCOHOL: Prohibited in public areas in every state park but may be consumed within the confines of a rented cabin, cabin site, lodge room, or campsite

VEHICLES: 2/site; no parking on grass or along edge of road

OTHER: Tents only; maximum 6 people/site; cutting or collecting of firewood prohibited; do not attach clotheslines to trees

Salt Fork's primitive campground was once a collection of small picnic areas. Because the location is off the main road and away from the major attractions of the park, park managers decided to transform the quiet ridge into five small groups of spacious tent-only campsites—spread out on what the park calls Bigfoot Ridge. The sites require a short walk from a paved parking area. The longest distance from parking to campsite is only 40 yards. Entering the primitive camping area, a picnic area remains on the left side of the paved road. Immediately on the right is Primitive Camp (PC) 5, which hosts three sites dispersed on a small rise with a few trees. If camping with a few friends, your small group could have this section to yourselves.

Across the road and a dozen yards down the park road is PC4. This four-site section is tucked into the woods surrounding an open area that includes a pit toilet, a drinking fountain, and a dishwater disposal basin. Site 4 is the farthest from the road and most private. The terrain is slightly sloping under PC4, but it's not a problem. With the myriad trees and a few spreading shrubs, you should avoid pitching a large tent here.

Back across the road and next to PC5 is PC3. Its five sites are spread out across the peak of a wide ridge that slopes away from the road. Sites 1 and 5 are hidden from the road, offering the most privacy. The road leading through the primitive campground is seldom traveled, so road noise is not an issue. The only other motor sound you may hear comes from the boats cruising 2,952-acre Salt Fork Lake, which lies at the bottom of the ridge the campground is perched on. Because of the heavy forest cover, sneak peeks of the lake from this campground only happen when the deciduous trees have shed their leaves for the season.

Six hundred feet down and across the road from PC3 is PC 2. This section holds the most amenities of the primitive camp. The four sites of PC2 are situated in the four corners of the section, with pit toilets, a water fountain, and a dishwater basin in the center. The water fountain is located next to site 1, which is nearest to the road. With eight-site PC1 across the road, PC2 receives the most foot traffic from campers using the restroom and obtaining drinking water. PC2's site 3 overlooks a wooded ravine. Various species of wildlife roam to the ridgetop to meander around the campsites, so keep your camera handy and the snacks sealed away.

At the end of the dead-end road is PC1. Eight sites in two rows roll away from the parking area. At the end of the row on the right is site 4, which sits away from the rest by a few extra yards at the perimeter of the ridgeline. Although site 4 demands the longest walk with camping gear from the car, the touch of solitude gained is worth it. At the end of PC1's parking area is the Gibson Farm trailhead, a 0.3-mile out-and-back path that passes small caves and rock outcrops—the perfect habitat for the Ohio Grassman to hide in.

Salt Fork State Park: Primitive Campground

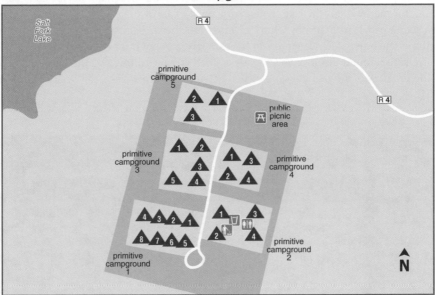

GETTING THERE

From I-77, take Exit 47, north of Cambridge, and follow US 22 east 6.4 miles to the park entrance on the left. Travel Park Road 1 for 4.6 miles to Park Road 4 on the left. Follow Park Road 4 for 0.7 mile and then bear left. Campground signage will be on the right after passing the paved parking area on the left.

GPS COORDINATES: N40° 07.526' W81° 30.420'

30

⛺ Strouds Run State Park

Beauty ★ Privacy ★★ Spaciousness ★★ Quiet ★★ Security ★★ Cleanliness ★★

Strouds Run State Park isn't far from town, but it still retains a wild flavor.

The drive to Strouds Run State Park includes a short jaunt through town and a few sharp turns and stops. For first-time visitors, the effort to find this little park may seem troublesome—until they arrive at the lake and then the campground. County Road 20 follows the shoreline of the upper end of 161-acre Dow Lake before leading to Township Road 212, which leads to the campground (signs are posted). One glance at the lake and you will want to pull over, throw out a picnic blanket, and soak up the atmosphere. The lake is surrounded by hardwood forest except for the northeast shoreline, which hosts a sandy beach and picnic area. During spring, summer, and fall, the lake is busy with small boats of anglers and paddlers—many of them young people from nearby Ohio University in Athens, the first college in the Northwest Territory. The college kids also frequent the campground, but in an orderly manner.

The campground lies in a valley with a small stream running at the base of the east hillside, and half of the sites are sandwiched between the stream and the campground road.

Hike to the overlook of Dow Lake at Strouds Run State Park.

KEY INFORMATION

LOCATION: 11661 State Park Road
Athens, Ohio 45701

CONTACT: The campground is operated
by a private concessionaire: 740-594-2628,
lakehillcabins.com/strouds-run; for questions
regarding the park, call Burr Oak State Park
at 740-767-3570 or visit parks.ohiodnr.gov
/stroudsrun#reserve

OPEN: Year-round

SITES: 78 nonelectric

EACH SITE HAS: Picnic table, fire ring

WHEELCHAIR ACCESS: None

ASSIGNMENT: First come, first served

REGISTRATION: At self-registration station
at campground entrance

AMENITIES: Pit toilets, drinking water,
dump station, playground, boat rentals

PARKING: At each site

FEE: $20 Apr.– Oct., $15 Nov.–Mar.

ELEVATION: 668 feet

RESTRICTIONS

PETS: On leash only, maximum 2 pets/site

QUIET HOURS: 10 p.m.–7 a.m.

FIRES: In fire ring

ALCOHOL: Prohibited

VEHICLES: 2/site

OTHER: Gathering firewood prohibited;
must register before occupying site;
no ATVs; must be age 18 or over to register
for campsite

The sites on the other side of the campground road have TR 212 to their backs. Normally a quiet road, TR 212 doesn't cause too much distraction from quiet camping. Most of the sites are shaded, with sections of sunshine beaming through during midday. Sites 1 and 2 receive full sun, while sites 17–20 have plenty of shade and ample space so that neighboring campers aren't too close for comfort. A drinking water spigot is located at site 25. After reaching the cul-de-sac and heading back out, sites 40–42 on the right are near the access for the Vista Point Trail. The trail is tough at times, but the view overlooking Dow Lake is worth the trip—don't forget to add the camera to the daypack. The trailhead for the Vista Point Trail is accessible near the amphitheater on the left as you pull into the campground. A footbridge crosses Labath Run and soon ascends to the overlook. Also, keep an eye out for the Indian mound 0.95 mile from the trailhead.

A small store near the boat ramp on Dow Lake (0.25 mile from the campground entrance) handles boat rentals, as well as ice cream for refueling paddlers on return from a cruise on the lake. The fishing in Dow Lake varies in species and access. Most of the lake's edges are steep and inaccessible by foot, but the Lakeview Trail does put adventurous anglers in position at several points to make a few casts. Access this trail from the southern point of the parking area on the east shore. Another path, the multiuse Hickory Trail, begins at the point where TR 212 turns off CR 20 and travels west 0.83 mile to the parking area on the left. The 3-mile trail is shared by hikers and bikers, but hikers predominate. Tie a 3-inch plastic, chartreuse twister tail grub onto 12-pound test line spooled onto a spinning reel and you're set for several species of game fish. Rainbow trout are stocked in the lake each spring. Locals work the lake pretty hard for the first week following the stocking, but a few hundred of the trout go deep and can be caught occasionally for a couple of months afterward. Healthy trout definitely make a fine camp dinner.

Strouds Run State Park

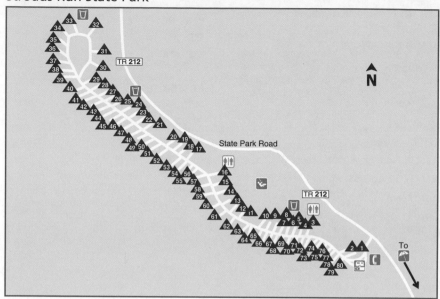

GETTING THERE

From Athens, follow US 33 northwest and take the OH 13/OH 550 (Chauncey/Amesville) exit. At the traffic light, turn left onto Columbus Road. Travel 2 miles to North Lancaster Street and turn left. Go 0.2 mile and bear right onto Columbia Avenue. Travel 1.1 miles to CR 20/Stroud's Run Road, turn right, and go 0.4 mile to the dead end. Turn right to remain on Stroud's Run Road and drive 3.1 miles to TR 212. Turn left and drive 0.1 mile to the campground entrance on the left.

GPS COORDINATES: N39° 21.305' W82° 02.378'

31

⚠ Tar Hollow State Park

Beauty ★★★ Privacy ★★★ Spaciousness ★★ Quiet ★★★ Security ★★★★ Cleanliness ★★★

Ohio's third-largest state forest surrounds Tar Hollow State Park.

Various points of access allow easy exploration of Tar Hollow State Park and State Forest, one of Ohio's best wilderness areas. Campers can explore the deep ravines and dense woodlands on 24 miles of hiking trails, 21 miles of backpacking trails, and 2.5 miles of mountain bike trails. Seventeen miles of paved roads and 14 miles of gravel roads offer scenic views of Ohio's third-largest state forest (more than 16,000 acres). The abundance of shortleaf and pitch pines growing on the ridges were once a source of pine tar for early settlers, the source of the park's name.

Spending one night in Tar Hollow's forests creates the desire for at least one more. The campground's deep woodland environment, enhanced with plenty of access via roads and trails, makes the park a camper's multiday retreat. There is truly not a bad site in any of the six camping locations. Driving west on Tar Hollow Road from OH 327, the first campground option is on the left in 1.2 miles. Nine sites encircle a stone parking area at the base of 15-acre Pine Lake's dam. The lake's spillway delivers a trickle of water regularly, but it picks up volume during rains. The released water doesn't impact the camping area, as the water is contained in a 5-yard-wide ditch. The sites closest to the dam, sites 87, 88, and 95,

North Ridge Walk-In Campground offers out-of-the-way, primitive camping at Tar Hollow State Park.

KEY INFORMATION

LOCATION: 16396 Tar Hollow Road
Laurelville, Ohio 43135

CONTACT: 740-887-4818,
parks.ohiodnr.gov/tarhollow

OPEN: Year-round; limited amenities in winter
(heated showers closed January–March)

SITES: 5 backpack, 23 nonelectric
(12 walk-in only), 68 electric

EACH SITE HAS: Picnic table, fire ring

WHEELCHAIR ACCESS: None

ASSIGNMENT: Walk-in sites first come, first
served; others may be reserved at 866-644-
6727 or ohiostateparks.reserveamerica.com

REGISTRATION: At general store (log cabin);
self-registration information posted outside
store

AMENITIES: Showers, flush toilets, laundry,
camp store, boat ramp, swimming beach,
bike rentals, boat rentals, game room,
minigolf, nature center

PARKING: At each site; parking area for
walk-in sites

FEE: $21 nonelectric, $28 electric, $5/adult for
backpack sites; deduct $3 in winter

ELEVATION: 814 feet

RESTRICTIONS

PETS: On leash only

QUIET HOURS: 10 p.m.–7 a.m.

FIRES: In fire ring, which must not be moved

ALCOHOL: Prohibited in public areas in every
state park but may be consumed within the
confines of a rented cabin, cabin site, lodge
room, or campsite

VEHICLES: 2/site; overflow parking at
adjacent lots

OTHER: Gathering firewood prohibited;
maximum 6 people/site

---

fill first on weekends. A moderate walk up the mowed grass–covered dam offers decent fishing. These sites are nonelectric, well spaced, and partially shaded.

Travel 0.45 mile farther on Tar Hollow Road to locate the beach (with one campsite between the beach and a picnic area), general store (camper registration and free Wi-Fi), minigolf, and bike and boat rentals. This is the hub of activity and information for the campgrounds, especially for camping families staying in the two main campgrounds just ahead. Across the road from the beach entrance are two sites sitting back in a small, wooded cove—rightly named the General Cove sites. The next right off Tar Hollow Road leads to Logan Hollow Campground. Its 41 electric sites, the most rustic of the 71 electric sites at Tar Hollow State Park, are stretched out along the narrow valley with steep ridges rising up on both sides. The sites on the left going in (38–50) sit along a stream that keeps cool thanks to the heavy tree canopy overhead. A short spur road off the Logan Hollow road holds sites 67–71. These five sites offer a quiet option if the main sections get busy.

In the next hollow over from Logan Hollow is Ross Hollow Campground. All 27 electric sites have paved parking pads and are normally taken by RVs. A heated shower house sets at the entrance to this section.

Back on Tar Hollow Road, travel 1.2 miles up a windy, narrow section of the road, which is also called Park Road 10. At the top of a ridge (330 feet higher in elevation) overlooking the main campgrounds is the North Ridge Walk-In Campground. The drive up the mountain to this remote-style campground may give the impression the road leads to nowhere, but the destination is one any tent camper will appreciate. Twelve sites encircle a 1-acre clearing on the peak of the forested ridge. The sites could be enhanced with a few more yards between them, but since this campground is so out of the way, it goes somewhat unnoticed, and that's a good thing. The first site is only a few yards from the gravel parking area and bulletin board. Sites 101–106 are the cream of the crop, with autumn and spring views of distant ridges that are filled with dew clouds in the mornings. The other six sites are strung along the lower side of the clearing, but they're still worthy because of the sense of serenity felt there.

For a camping experience even deeper in the forest, follow the park road out to South Ridge Road (Park Road 3), turn left, and drive south 1.5 miles to the fire tower. East of the fire tower parking area are five backpack sites, just out of sight on the opposite side of a small pit toilet. The North Country Trail, which follows about 800 miles of the Buckeye Trail, passes through the park at this point using Tar Hollow's Logan Trail. If you hike any of Tar Hollow's trails, keep an eye out for timber rattlesnakes. The rattlers are at home on the dry, rocky ridgetops of the park. Timber rattlers are found in only seven counties in Ohio, and Tar Hollow lies in three of those counties.

Tar Hollow State Park

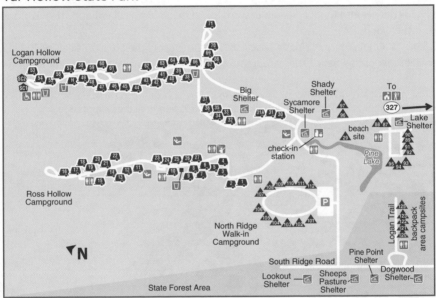

GETTING THERE

From Adelphi, travel 7.4 miles south on OH 327 to the park entrance on the right.

GPS COORDINATES: N39° 23.018' W82° 44.777'

32

⛺ Wolf Run State Park

Beauty ★★★ Privacy ★★ Spaciousness ★★ Quiet ★★ Security ★★★ Cleanliness ★★★

This quiet, beautiful park is conveniently located near the interstate.

Wolf Run State Park lies in northern Noble County, which is tagged as The Gateway to Appalachia by the visitors bureau. The foothills of this region offer an abundance of outdoors adventures. The 1,406-acre state park is only a couple of miles from the interstate, but the sights and sounds of a bustling highway quickly vanish once you're inside the park. The surrounding forests are the result of restoration efforts performed in the 1930s. The current forest floor is home to a variety of species of ferns, mosses, and fungi. You can get an up-close look at this healthy forest environment from a 2.5-mile stretch of the Buckeye Trail that follows the lake's western shoreline. The path wanders from the shoreline occasionally and heads deeper into the forest—an eastern forest field guide will enhance this explorative walk in the woods.

Using Wolf Run State Park as a base camp while touring the area, tent campers will find three sections of this neat little campground sitting as a crown atop five adjoining finger

Some of the tent sites at Wolf Run State Park are only a few steps from the water's edge.

KEY INFORMATION

LOCATION: Caldwell

CONTACT: 740-732-5035,
parks.ohiodnr.gov/wolfrun

OPEN: Year-round; heated shower and water
open in winter

SITES: 65 nonelectric, 72 electric

EACH SITE HAS: Picnic table, fire ring

WHEELCHAIR ACCESS: No specific
ADA-accessible sites

ASSIGNMENT: Walk-in sites first come, first
served; others may be reserved at 866-644-
6727 or ohiostateparks.reserveamerica.com

REGISTRATION: At camp store; self-
registration station on front of camp store

AMENITIES: Camp store, showers, flush and
pit toilets, laundry, playground, sports

courts, boat ramp, nature center,
swimming beach

PARKING: At each site

FEE: $22 nonelectric, $26 electric;
deduct $3 in winter

ELEVATION: 890 feet

RESTRICTIONS

PETS: On leash only

QUIET HOURS: 10 p.m.–7 a.m.

FIRES: In fire ring, which must not be moved

ALCOHOL: Prohibited in public areas in every
state park but may be consumed within the
confines of a rented cabin, cabin site, lodge
room, or campsite

VEHICLES: 2/site

OTHER: Gathering firewood prohibited; most
supplies available in Caldwell

ridges. After a quick stop at the camp store/registration center, you will likely see RVs at the sites straight ahead. Turn right at the intersection and follow the main campground road past two sections of sites on the left, then follow the road around and down a long hill to the best tent sites of Wolf Run. At the bottom of the hill and at the lake's edge are sites 22–26, called premium lakeside sites—and they are. These five sites have panoramic views of the picturesque lake and are only a few steps from the water's edge. The sites are roomy enough for a larger tent, but with such a pretty lake environment, you'll spend little time in the tent. The lake has a 10-horsepower limit, so you can paddle without the concern of overcoming 3-foot wakes. While sitting at your site at sunrise and sunset, you may spot a great blue heron wading in the shallows in search of food. Rainbow trout are released into the lake each March, which draws a decent number of anglers. From this group of sites, the 1.1-mile Lakeview Trail leads to the beach east of the campground.

Traveling back up the hill on the main campground road, sites 27–36 are on the right and situated along the rim of a lake cove. These sites are sloping but manageable for tent camping. A steep walk from each site through the forested banks will lead to the lake. Across the road from site 30 are a drinking water spigot and pit toilet. Once on top of the hill, take the branch to the right between sites 44 and 67. Go to the cul-de-sac to find sites 51–56, which are a bit tight but can accommodate a four-person tent. During green leaf season, the lake is hidden by vegetation, but in early spring and fall, you'll enjoy views of the lake and more breezes. A pit toilet is near site 56, and a shower house is located between sites 45 and 46, which you passed on the right after turning onto the branch road. This shower house is the closer of the two in the campground to the sites highlighted so far.

Return to the main campground road and go straight to a cul-de-sac surrounded by sites 126–133. You will pass a group of sites on the right getting to that point that is usually filled with RVs. Sites 126–133 have an overlook of the lake and dam. They're not especially spacious, but the view is worth the effort to fit your tent onto the site. These spots are mostly sunny, but westerly winds keep them fresh.

For a peek at some history that has affected everyone, jump back on I-77 and go south to Exit 25. Drive 1.8 miles east on OH 78 to the junction of OH 564. There you will find the first oil well in North America. It's a historical site that is protected by a fence, but you can view it. The well, created in 1814, is still lined with a hollow sycamore log that is visible sticking up above the well today. A historical marker on site tells the rest of the story.

Wolf Run State Park

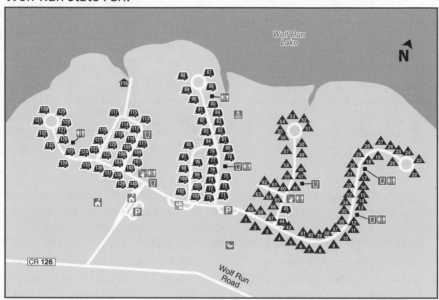

GETTING THERE

From I-77, take Exit 28 in Belle Valley and go south on OH 821 for 0.4 mile to OH 215. Turn left and travel 0.9 mile to County Road 126. Turn left and go 0.3 mile to the park entrance on the right.

GPS COORDINATES: N39° 47.3742' W81° 32.4297'

SOUTHWEST

The gently sloped campsites at John Bryan State Park (see page 120) are perfect for tent campers.

33

⛺ Germantown Metropark

Beauty ★★★ Privacy ★★★★ Spaciousness ★★★★ Quiet ★★★★ Security ★★★ Cleanliness ★★★

Spend a night immersed in this park's beautiful landscape.

Only 20 minutes from Dayton, this chunk of wilderness contains deep, scenic ravines and Twin Creek, a tributary of the Great Miami River. A dam on Twin Creek controls any flooding issues and offers a great view of the park. Fossil-hunting is permitted below the dam, and you can launch your canoe there too—just follow the signage. The 2,665-acre Germantown Metropark is a natural icon for many children of the region who visit frequently on field trips. You can explore the park on foot via 16 miles of hiking trails, or drive the paved park road that courses through an old-growth forest featuring clean Twin Creek. The park road is on the west side of Conservancy Road, just north of the dam, and has several pull-over areas that lead to a fishing pond and a scenic overlook.

Spending a night immersed in the metropark's beautiful landscape is icing on the camper's adventure cake. There are two options for car camping, and both offer a rare method of doing so, as there are no individual sites; instead, there's only one open site with a 6-foot-wide steel fire ring in the center of the camping area. On the eastern side of the metropark is Old Mill Campsite, not far from the Germantown Dam. A small, paved parking area that can handle only four vehicles is next to Old Mill Road. Also in the parking area is a small firewood supply shed, with free firewood for campers' use. Across the road from the parking area is a signpost marking the crossing of the Twin Valley Trail (TVT). The TVT is a backpacking trail that connects Germantown Metropark with Twin Creek Metropark to the south.

At Germantown, you'll find easy access for paddling Twin Creek, which leads to the Great Miami River.

KEY INFORMATION

LOCATION: 7173 Old Mill Road
Germantown, Ohio 45327

CONTACT: Operated by Five Rivers
Metroparks: 937-275-7275, metroparks.org

OPEN: Year-round

SITES: 1 large shared site

EACH SITE HAS: Picnic table, center fire ring

WHEELCHAIR ACCESS: None

ASSIGNMENT: Must reserve a permit at least
4 days in advance at 937-275-7275 or
metroparks.org

REGISTRATION: Print permit at home and
keep on person during visit

AMENITIES: Pit toilet, firewood supply (fee),
nature center with water available

PARKING: Parking area at campground

FEE: Nov.–Mar. $18 weekdays, $25 weekends;
Apr.–Oct. $25 weekdays, $35 weekends

ELEVATION: Old Mill Campsite, 759 feet;
Shimps Hollow Group Camp, 913 feet

RESTRICTIONS

PETS: On leash only

FIRES: In fire ring

ALCOHOL: Prohibited

VEHICLES: At parking area

OTHER: Firewood provided (do not bring it
with you); no amplified music

Down a small and slight slope from the parking area is the one large campsite measuring approximately 75 feet by 100 feet. On the north side of the grassy campsite is a set of wood steps leading up to a pit toilet. The campsite is surrounded by forest and a creek on the far east side. The large fire ring, sitting near the campsite's center, invites campers to sit a spell on the two log benches appropriately positioned within a roasting stick's length away from the fire. Two picnic tables are also located on the big site and usually go to the first arrivals. If you're the only camper at the site, then you have plenty of room to spread out as you wish. But if one or more additional parties join the fun, you will have to choose a corner or set up in the middle. A few trees help break up the site when multiple camps are needed. At the dead end of Old Mill Road is a picnic area that attracts day users. A trail leads from the picnic area for a loop hike through the Bob Siebenthaler Natural Area, a woodland offering many natural rewards thanks to intensive forest stewardship.

The second site at Germantown is Shimps Hollow Group Camp, located in the southwest corner of the property, off Boomershine Road. A gravel lane runs about a quarter mile from the road to the campsite parking area. This site also has one large fire ring, five picnic tables, and a pit toilet near the parking area. The site itself is approximately 75 feet by 400 feet and sprawls out under mature trees. Although this area is called a group camp, individual campers may use the site if it's not fully reserved. Shimps Hollow sits at the edge and center of two hollows, hence the name. Both wooded hollows lead deep into the park toward the Orange Trail, a 6.8-mile hiking trail. If you only have time to hike one of the seven existing trails in the park, this is the one. A good place to start your hike on the Orange Trail is at the extraordinary nature center, just north of Shimps Hollow on Boomershine Road. From there, the Orange Trail drops over the edge of the creek valley, which runs north, and passes the northern boundary of the park before turning south on the east side of the valley. The hardwood forest clinging to the sides of the creek valley warrants frequent stops to look up and admire, so plan to spend a full day hiking this trail. The path turns west at the dam and then north again. But before you make it back to the nature center, you will have walked through one of the oldest surviving forests today. Take many photos of the old-growth forest, as you may not see such a display of nature in Ohio again.

Germantown Metropark

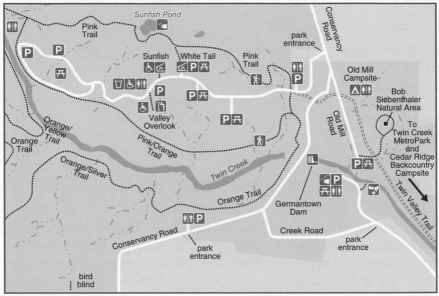

GETTING THERE

From Germantown, follow OH 725 west 2.3 miles. Turn right on Conservancy Road and travel 1.6 miles north to Old Mill Road. Turn right and follow Old Mill Road 0.15 mile to Old Mill Campsite on the left.

GPS COORDINATES

Old Mill Campsite: N39° 38.360' W84° 23.991'
Shimps Hollow Group Camp: N39° 37.962' W84° 25.857'

34

⚑ Great Seal State Park

Beauty ★★★ Privacy ★★ Spaciousness ★★★ Quiet ★★ Security ★★ Cleanliness ★★★

Great Seal features a range of majestic hills dotted with thousands of years of Shawnee Indian history.

Driving toward Chillicothe from any direction except the east, a group of tall foothills runs north to south like a miniature mountain range greeting visitors—this is Great Seal State Park. The park's name comes from the state's emblem, The Great Seal of the State of Ohio. The several hills that are depicted in the emblem are the ones that create the state park. The hills stand majestically above the till plains to the west and north and provide a gateway to the Appalachian Region to the south and east. The region is full of American Indian history, and the numerous historical sites that populate the area offer a clear look at an impressive culture. Big hills, rivers, and flatlands that have sustained life for centuries continue to provide a place for visitors to connect with the natural world.

Halfway up Sugarloaf Mountain, rounded up like circled wagons, are the 15 sites that complete the small campground. This campground is favored by equestrians, but if you camp here during the week, you typically won't see any horses (or other people) milling about. Inside the campground loop are a shelter house and picnic area. Sites 1–10 are spread

Campfire stew is a treat.   *Photo by Hypatia Luna*

KEY INFORMATION

LOCATION: 4908 Marietta Road
Chillicothe, Ohio 45601

CONTACT: 740-887-4818 (Tar Hollow
State Park handles this park's calls),
parks.ohiodnr.gov/greatseal

OPEN: March–November

SITES: 15 nonelectric

EACH SITE HAS: Picnic table, fire ring

WHEELCHAIR ACCESS: None

ASSIGNMENT: First come, first served

REGISTRATION: Self-registration station at
campground entrance

AMENITIES: Pit toilet, water supply,
playground

PARKING: At each site

FEE: $20

ELEVATION: 867 feet

RESTRICTIONS

PETS: On leash only

QUIET HOURS: 10 p.m.–7 a.m.

FIRES: In fire ring

ALCOHOL: Prohibited in public areas in every
state park but may be consumed within the
confines of a rented cabin, cabin site, lodge
room, or campsite

VEHICLES: 2/site

OTHER: Gathering firewood prohibited;
maximum 6 people/site

widely around the entire campground loop road. The campground covers approximately 4 acres of closely mowed lawn, with a few trees here and there, and the outer sites are situated on the outer edges of the clearing. Sites 11–15 are on the inside of the loop, starting near the picnic shelter. These five sites are in full sun all day. As the loop makes the turn at the top of the slope, sites 6 and 7 are hidden in a few yards of shade from three oak trees, as well as the trees surrounding the open meadow. Each site has a gravel parking pad that can easily hold two vehicles, as the sites were built to accommodate a horse trailer and tow vehicle. Running along the back side of sites 1–10 is a picket line for tethering horses. Park managers enforce strict rules for owners to clean up after their animals, which most equestrians consider a given in their unspoken code of trail-riding ethics.

A pit toilet and water spigot are only a few yards from the self-registration station. Also near the station is a trailhead sign calling out the three trails accessible from that point: 0.8-mile Sugarloaf Mountain Trail with yellow blazes, 6.3-mile Shawnee Ridge Trail with blue blazes, and 1.6-mile Mount Ives Trail with orange blazes. All of the trails roaming the hills of Great Seal State Park are categorized as strenuous. Sugarloaf Mountain Trail rises to the peak of the mountain, leading hikers on a 500-foot ascent in less than a quarter mile. Be sure to carry a park map to help you navigate the colorful blazes throughout the park. Trail trekking is the main adventure here, and several of the trails are multiuse, allowing hikers, equestrians, and mountain bikers. At the eastern base of Sugarloaf Mountain is the site of the outdoor historical drama *Tecumseh!*, performed June–early September at the Sugarloaf Mountain Amphitheater. For more American Indian history, visit the Hopewell Culture National Historical Park for hours of learning. The park is located 1 mile north of Chillicothe on OH 104. Walk among 23 earthen mounds and view artifacts discovered on the protected property displayed in the museum. A stroll along the Scioto River, which flows along the park's eastern boundary, demands a few minutes of pause to let your mind consider what life was like here a few hundred years ago.

Great Seal State Park

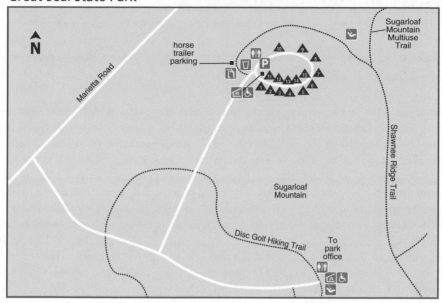

GETTING THERE

From Chillicothe, follow OH 159 north 4.2 miles to Delano Road. Turn right and travel 1 mile to Marietta Road. Turn right and travel south 0.8 mile to the park entrance on the left. Follow signage to the first left and the campground.

GPS COORDINATES: N39° 24.139' W82° 56.474'

35

⛺ John Bryan State Park

Beauty ★★★ Privacy ★★★ Spaciousness ★★★ Quiet ★★★ Security ★★★★ Cleanliness ★★★

Clifton Gorge, cut by the Little Miami State and National Scenic River, serves as the backdrop for this 752-acre park.

John Bryan State Park is not only scenic, with several geographical features for sightseers, but it's also an attraction for avid hikers, mountain bikers, and cliff clingers. The gorges cut by the Little Miami River are skirted by trails with photo-worthy views, as well as challenging rock climbing and repelling for extreme outdoors adventurers. With so much to do in and around the Clifton Gorge area, a base camp is necessary to catch some rest before rising to head down the next trail. Before heading home, be sure to drive or stroll through nearby Yellow Springs, a unique little town with widespread displays of artworks of all kinds.

The campground at John Bryan lacks some common facilities, such as showers, but tent campers will appreciate its simplicity. The entrance passes through a split rail fence, and the campground lies over a rolling hill like a saddle on a horse. Halfway to the top of the hill, on the right, are sites 1–11. Half of those sites are downhill, while the other half lie on the upslope from the camp road. The slope is mostly open except for a few deciduous trees providing a hint of shade. The lower sites are nearly as wide as they are long, with lots of space for a big tent with comfy cots.

A fawn rests in the grass on a sunny morning at John Bryan State Park.

KEY INFORMATION

LOCATION: 3790 OH 370
Yellow Springs, Ohio 45387-9743

CONTACT: 937-767-1274,
parks.ohiodnr.gov/johnbryan

OPEN: Year-round; limited facilities in winter

SITES: 52 nonelectric, 9 electric

EACH SITE HAS: Picnic table, fire ring

WHEELCHAIR ACCESS: No specific
ADA-accessible sites

ASSIGNMENT: Walk-in sites first come, first
served; others may be reserved at 866-644-
6727 or ohiostateparks.reserveamerica.com

REGISTRATION: Self-registration station
at campground office, if campground
office closed

AMENITIES: Pit toilets, potable water,
camp store, disc-golf course, sports courts,
playground, canoe launch nearby

PARKING: At each site

FEE: $23 electric, $19 nonelectric

ELEVATION: 999 feet

RESTRICTIONS

PETS: On leash only

QUIET HOURS: 10 p.m.–7 a.m.

FIRES: In fire ring, which must not be moved

ALCOHOL: Prohibited in public areas in every
state park but may be consumed within the
confines of a rented cabin, cabin site, lodge
room, or campsite

VEHICLES: 2/site

OTHER: Gathering firewood prohibited;
maximum 6 people/site

At the turn of the long looping lane, sites 13, 15, and 17 sit halfway in the edge of thick forest. Sites 19, 21, and 23 are next in line before the loop finishes the turn. Site 23 is especially inviting, with ample space and the aroma of oaks, which are the primary trees throughout the campground. The only caveat is OH 370 sneaks by in those woods, only a dozen yards away, so you might hear some traffic noise. The sites on the top of the hill have wide views of the campground. RVers migrate to those sites, which keeps them corralled primarily in one spot. However, most campers at John Bryan State Park are tenters enjoying more than one day exploring the gorge.

The lane that ushers you into the campground cuts through the heart of it and, after cresting the hill, then snakes left and right as it escapes into the forest skirting the west side of the campground. Before the road enters the deeper forest, five sites flank a short lane. Site 67 rests against the woods, and from that point you can't see the majority of the campground and the campground can't see you; it offers a touch of privacy except for the lane, which is also used by park personnel coming and going from a maintenance building hidden in the woods. Sites 53–61 are east of site 67 and accessed from another looping lane opposite the first, larger one. Sites 57 and 59 offer the most space with an open lawn area. At the middle of this loop is a smaller, connecting loop with sites 41–49. Sites 45 and 47 are on the outside of the little loop and near the edge of a steep ravine that steers the Little Miami River, 150 feet below. On breezy days, these sites catch a refreshing draft filtering up from the valley. A trail leads away near site 43, descends the ravine, and arrives at the parking area of the lower picnic area. From there, a network of trails follows the river gorge for 2 miles.

From the campground entrance, take a right and then a left, bypass the day-use lodge on the left, and pull over and park at the Wingo Picnic Area. Snug up the hiking boots and hit the trail that leaves from the south side of the picnic area and soon joins the North Rim

Trail. This will put you in the middle of the rock climbing and repelling area to either rope up or simply observe.

John Bryan State Park

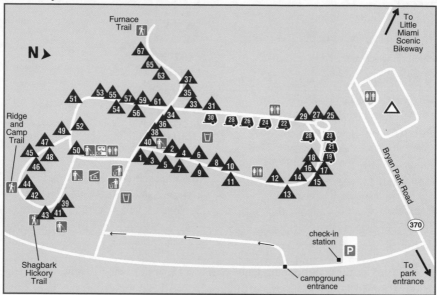

GETTING THERE

From I-70 near Springfield, take Exit 52 and follow US 68 south 6.6 miles to OH 343. Turn left at the traffic light and go east 1 mile to OH 370/Bryan Park Road. Turn right and travel south 1.1 miles to the park entrance on the left. The campground office is 500 feet ahead.

GPS COORDINATES: N39° 47.348' W83° 51.955'

36

⛺ Miami Whitewater Forest

Beauty ★★★ Privacy ★★★ Spaciousness ★★ Quiet ★★★ Security ★★★★ Cleanliness ★★★

This recreational retreat is only 30 minutes from Cincinnati, but it has none of the metro mayhem.

The 4,160-acre Miami Whitewater Forest has it all: access to fishing, boat and bike rentals, a 7.8-mile hike-and-bike trail, an 18-hole championship golf course and driving range, a water park, an 85-acre lake, and nature trails. This natural retreat is truly a destination camping option. Within a few minutes, campers can shed their mental baggage of daily stressors and begin to renew their outlook on what matters.

You wouldn't think a quiet camping place could be possible within a few miles of a metropolitan area and in a busy county park, but it exists at Miami Whitewater Forest. A cone-shaped hill rises 100 feet to the west of the heart of the park—the lake with the same name as the park—and supports 46 campsites from the top to the bottom. Even at the peak of park visitation in midsummer, the campground remains a quiet retreat with some vacancies. The paved, one-way loop lane heads uphill at the campground entrance. Sites flank both sides of the road that covers nearly a half mile through the forested hill.

Sites 101–110 sit on the upslope on individual shelves of gravel parking pads and small open areas that can accommodate a medium-size tent at best. As the campground lane nears the peak, site 113 on the right is the last site on that side until the lane winds around

A compact and cozy site at Miami Whitewater Forest

Photo courtesy of Hamilton County Parks

KEY INFORMATION

LOCATION: 9001 Mt. Hope Road
Harrison, Ohio 45030

CONTACT: Operated by Hamilton County Park
District: 513-851-2267, greatparks.org

OPEN: March–October

SITES: 46 electric

EACH SITE HAS: Picnic table, fire ring

WHEELCHAIR ACCESS: No specific
ADA-accessible sites

ASSIGNMENT: First come, first served and by
reservation at 513-851-2267 or greatparks.org

REGISTRATION: At the visitor center

AMENITIES: Showers, flush toilets, nature
center at visitor center, boat rentals,
disc-golf course, 18-hole golf course,
playground, wet playground

PARKING: At each site

FEE: $30.50 weekdays, $33.50 weekends;
Daily Resident MVP (park pass) $3,
nonresident $5

ELEVATION: 609 feet

RESTRICTIONS

PETS: Maximum 2/site

QUIET HOURS: 10 p.m.–9 a.m.

FIRES: In fire ring; bringing own firewood
prohibited; firewood available at visitor
center for a fee

ALCOHOL: Prohibited

VEHICLES: 2/site

OTHER: Cutting trees for firewood prohibited;
at least one member of camping party must
be age 18 or older.

and descends 40 yards to the lower level and the remainder of the sites. But across the lane from site 113 are sites 114 and 115. These three sites offer views to the east and west when the leaves have shed for the year and also receive a refreshing, steady breeze. These higher sites receive the least amount of occupancy, making them the most laid-back.

The entire hill is covered with a young, deciduous forest, which echoes constantly with songbirds in spring, summer, and fall. Birders will develop sore neck muscles from following the little avian creatures darting from tree to tree, while belting out their tunes. Site 116 is the first site on the right after arriving at the lower level of the campground; it requires a 10-yard walk from the parking pad to the site, which gives some privacy from the next site and the lane. From that point on around to the last site, the sites on the outer, right side of the looping lane are backed by a safety fence, which keeps campers from falling over a cliff and into Dry Fork Creek. Site 128 is not very deep because of its proximity to the fence. Sites 138–144 become a little close, so expect to trade camping stories or the day's adventures with your neighbors. The last two sites, 145 and 146, sit on each side of the lane and open up with a bit more space and no neighbors on the exit side. Back at the campground entrance is a modern, updated shower house with flush toilets, a potable water spigot, and a bulletin board.

Turn right out of the campground, return to Timberlakes Drive, and go left. Along the road you will see paved pullovers, but stop at the Timberlakes Program Shelter on the left near the top of the ridge. From there, you can access a nature trail with interpretive stations. The park district maintains an extensive nature conservation program, with the many results found along this and other nature trails of the park. When registering for your campsite at the visitor center, be sure to grab a trail map as well.

Miami Whitewater Forest Campground

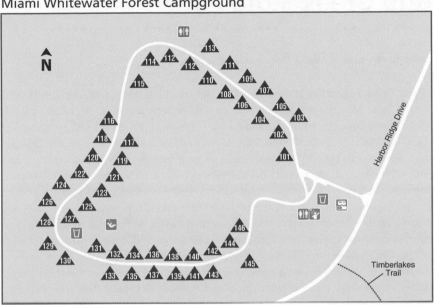

GETTING THERE

From the west side of Cincinnati, take I-74 to Exit 3. Travel north 0.9 mile on Dry Fork Road and turn right on West Road. Follow West Road 0.25 mile and turn left on Timberlakes Drive. Travel 0.6 mile to Harbor Ridge Drive and turn left. The campground entrance is ahead on the left.

GPS COORDINATES: N39° 15.383' W84° 44.873'

37

⛺ Paint Creek State Park

Beauty ★★★ Privacy ★★ Spaciousness ★★★ Quiet ★★ Security ★★★★ Cleanliness ★★★★

Welcome to the edge of Ohio's Appalachian Plateau.

The Paint Creek region lies at the edge of the Appalachian Plateau, marking the boundary between Ohio's hilly eastern section and its flat western segment. At 1,200 acres, Paint Creek Lake is a huge attraction at Paint Creek State Park, but there's still much to explore surrounding the park. Seip Mound State Memorial lies 2.8 miles east of Bainbridge. The mound, over 30 feet tall and 240 feet long, was built by Hopewell Indians starting around 100 BC. Descriptive signage on site details the ways of the ancient people who once thrived throughout the region. For more information, visit stateparks.com/seip_mound_state_memorial_in_ohio.html. South of the park on Cave Road, 1.36 miles from US 50, are the Highlands Nature Sanctuary and the Appalachian Forest Museum (arcofappalachia.org). Explore 14 miles of hiking trails through a rocky gorge and a forest with rare trees and plants; it's like walking through the wild Ohio of centuries ago.

Sitting atop a split peninsula coming out from Paint Creek Lake's eastern shore is a modern campground. It's as clean a camping facility as I've seen. Park friends are active

Paint Creek State Park features spacious sites and manicured lawns.

KEY INFORMATION

LOCATION: 280 Taylor Road
Bainbridge, Ohio 45612

CONTACT: 937-981-7061 (seasonal camp
office), 937-393-4284 (off season);
parks.ohiodnr.gov/paintcreek

OPEN: Year-round; limited facilities in winter,
but shower house and water available

SITES: 198 electric; primitive equestrian camp

EACH SITE HAS: Picnic table, fire ring

WHEELCHAIR ACCESS: Sites 13 and 15 and
shower house are ADA-accessible.

ASSIGNMENT: Walk-in sites first come,
first served; others may be reserved at
866-644-6727 or ohiostateparks.reserve
america.com

REGISTRATION: At campground office;
self-register at office if closed

AMENITIES: Showers, flush toilets, laundry,
camp store, game room, boat ramp, boat
rentals, disc-golf course, minigolf,
swimming beach

PARKING: At each site

FEE: $28; deduct $3 in winter

ELEVATION: 910 feet

RESTRICTIONS

PETS: On leash only; maximum 2 pets

QUIET HOURS: 10 p.m.–7 a.m.

FIRES: In fire ring, which must not be moved

ALCOHOL: Prohibited in public areas in every
state park but may be consumed within the
confines of a rented cabin, cabin site, lodge
room, or campsite

VEHICLES: 2/site; overflow parking near
camp store

OTHER: Gathering firewood prohibited;
maximum 6 people/site

year-round at the park and it shows. At first glance, the place appears to be a trendy, modern campground with paved pads and manicured lawns. But after spending a few minutes touring around, you'll find that it's a quiet, well-maintained campground that sees a split share of tent campers and RVers mixed throughout. A fully stocked camp store is the first stop at the entrance to the campground. With a wide variety of outdoor pursuits in which to partake, it's worth a brief visit with the employees at the store to get the scoop on current park events. Next to the camp store is a nature center that even the big kids will enjoy.

Camping Area One is on the right past the store and spreads out on the northern split of the peninsula. Sites 1–25 are popular with RVs. At the tip of Area One are several sites enhanced with wooden decks that overlook the lake. There are no designated trails leading from this point in the campground down to the lake. It's a steep drop from the campsites to the water, so ignore the urge to create a shortcut and instead access the lake from the numerous safe points. Of the six sites with decks in Area One, sites 37 and 38 are the only two that have ample space for pitching a tent. Following the area lane back to the main campground lane, site 57 on the right slopes a few yards downhill to the campsite, which sets it off by itself a little. Site 62 on the left, opposite a rental cabin, escapes the lawnlike camping theme that describes most of the central sites and features a small woodlot. A walk past three sites west of site 62 brings you to a shower house and drinking water.

The main campground lane leading from Area One to Areas Two and Three has three sites on the right. Sites 67 and 69 offer a quiet setting at the bottom of a short slope. Swing right into Area Three and onto the longest section of the peninsula. Sites 78 and 80 are halfway to the peninsula's point. These two sites having parking pads at the road's edge, but the campsites are set in the woods 10 yards farther from the road. At the point are eight additional sites with decks also overlooking the lake. Of those sites, 113, 115, and 116 offer the most unobstructed views (even during summer) of the lake, and they also have space for a large tent. The lake and its forested shoreline are mesmerizing during the fall leaf-changing season. Area Two is shaped like a boot, and at the eastern tip of the toe section are sites 158 and 161. Both are spacious with a mix of shade and sun. Located at the back of the campground, they're out of sight of the heart of the action and peaceful.

Across the lake from the campground is the primitive equestrian camp. From US 50, follow Upp Road north 1.29 miles to find trailer parking and the camp on the left. Paint Creek is controlled by the U.S. Army Corps of Engineers. Visit their office, located near the Paint Creek Lake Dam off Rapid Forge Road south of Taylor Road, for current information concerning special water releases for kayaking Paint Creek. Rock climbing is available at the spillway wall and on the Harmony Trail, both accessible from the dam and spillway parking lots.

Paint Creek State Park

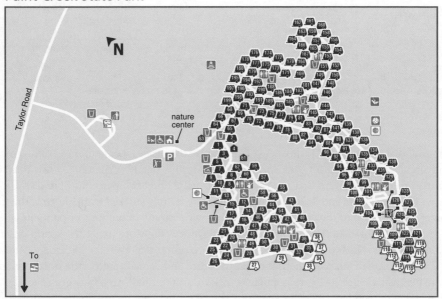

GETTING THERE

From Bainbridge, follow US 50 west 4 miles to Rapid Forge Road and turn right. Travel north 3.7 miles to Taylor Road and turn left. Follow Taylor Road west 0.7 mile to the park road on the left, which leads to the camp entrance.

GPS COORDINATES: N39° 16.226' W83° 22.750'

38

⚠ Pike Lake State Park

Beauty ★★★ Privacy ★★ Spaciousness ★★ Quiet ★★ Security ★★★ Cleanliness ★★★

This quaint, out-of-the-way little park is nestled among forested ridges.

The steep hills and shaded hollows of the area that now contains Pike Lake State Park and State Forest were heavily used by the armies fighting the Civil War. The rough land offered efficient hiding places to avoid conflict or to stage an ambush. Today the park region is a quiet and peaceful place to explore on land and water. The park sits in the center of the state forest, and 13-acre Pike Lake is center stage in the park. The roads leading to the park from the north are a bit rough, but you should drive slowly down Pike Lake Road (County Road 4) anyway to take in the scenic forestland.

Near the southwest corner of the lake, dug by the Civilian Conservation Corps in the 1930s, is a crossroads. On the north side of the crossroads is the park office, and next door to that is the camp store, which has all you'll need while camping at Pike Lake. If you didn't bring your canoe, you can rent one here. The lakeshore is just across the road to the east. About 100 yards west from the crossroads, following Egypt Hollow Road, you'll find the 0.5-mile Greenbrier Trail on the north side of the road. On the south side of Egypt Hollow Road, opposite the Greenbrier Trail, is the 0.5-mile CCC Trail. These well-defined, short hikes welcome children.

Pike Lake's raised sites help campers stay dry.

KEY INFORMATION

LOCATION: 1847 Pike Lake Road
Bainbridge, Ohio 45612

CONTACT: 740-493-2212,
parks.ohiodnr.gov/pikelake

OPEN: Year-round; limited facilities
in winter

SITES: 79 electric

EACH SITE HAS: Picnic table, fire ring

WHEELCHAIR ACCESS: No specific
ADA-accessible sites

ASSIGNMENT: Walk-in sites first come, first
served; others may be reserved at 866-644-
6727 or ohiostateparks.reserveamerica.com

REGISTRATION: Self-registration station at
campground entrance

AMENITIES: Pit toilets, water spigots, showers
at beach house, camp store, laundry, sports
courts, playground, swimming beach, canoe
rentals, disc-golf course, fishing pier

PARKING: At each site

FEE: $24; deduct $3 in winter

ELEVATION: 749 feet

RESTRICTIONS

PETS: On leash only

QUIET HOURS: 10 p.m.–7 a.m.

FIRES: In fire ring, which must not be moved

ALCOHOL: Prohibited in public areas in every
state park but may be consumed within the
confines of a rented cabin, cabin site, lodge
room, or campsite

VEHICLES: 2/site

OTHER: Gathering firewood prohibited;
maximum 6 people/site

Also south of Egypt Hollow Road is the campground, which lies along the base of a long ridge in a woodland of medium-size trees that provide abundant shade during leaf season. At only 0.25 mile long and 0.8 mile wide, the campground doesn't have a huge footprint. Its 79 sites are strategically spotted throughout the rectangle, but it's not a busy place, so you can enjoy a quiet camp here. The campground is flat, and almost too flat in the center, as several sites stay moist during rains. A kiosk with self-registration materials greets campers. A dedicated group of friends of the state park regularly holds events open to all campers, and these are posted at the kiosk. Sites 1–23 parallel Pike Lake Road, and with no natural screening between the sites and the road, they do experience some traffic noise, but the road is not overly traveled. As the paved lane turns at the group camp's parking area, sites 24 and 25 are on the right. If the group camp is not occupied, these two sites offer the most serenity.

North of site 25, and 20 yards beyond the turn back toward the entrance and through the center of the campground, is site 57. This spot is both wide and deep and brushed with a mix of shade and sun. You can't go wrong with site 57. Follow the lane around to site 64, which resembles site 57's layout but has more trees. The valley floor remains a few degrees cooler thanks to the heavy forest covering the ridges and the breezes gliding across the lake's surface and filtering through the campground. Sites 66, 67, and 69 are the last of the most comfortable sites (in full shade) before arriving back at the campground entrance. A footbridge crosses a 4-yard-wide creek from the campground to the dam, which has a picnic area.

From the dam area, a paved pathway follows the lake's western shoreline and provides easy access for fishing and launching a canoe or kayak. Two fishing piers jut out into the lake from this paved pathway, which allows anglers in wheelchairs a good shot at largemouth bass in spring and fall and catfish in summer. On an island in the northern tip of the lake are a swimming beach and the shower house, which are accessible by a footbridge. Kayaking anglers may catch a few crappies for a tasty camp lunch in the early spring around this bridge. Pike Lake State Park is off the beaten path and at least a dozen miles from any other attraction. But with several miles of well-groomed trails and such a pretty little lake, there's plenty to see and do to fill a weekend at the park.

Pike Lake State Park

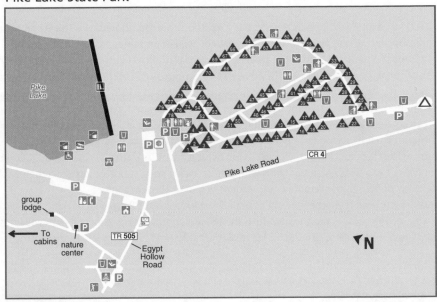

GETTING THERE

From Bainbridge, follow County Road 28 (Potts Hill Road) south 3.2 miles and turn right on CR 4. Follow CR 4 south 3.1 miles to the campground entrance on the left.

GPS COORDINATES: N39° 09.499' W83° 13.260'

39

⛺ Scioto Trail State Park:
HIKE-IN CAMPGROUND

Beauty ★★★ Privacy ★★★★ Spaciousness ★★★ Quiet ★★★ Security ★★ Cleanliness ★★★

The remote nature of this park means campers will spot an abundance of wildlife year-round.

Scioto Trail State Park sprawls among the forestland on the doorstep of the Appalachian foothills bordering the Scioto River. The paved, well-maintained roads leading into and throughout the park are somewhat steep and curvy but allow campers to explore the true nature of the park and state forest. There are two campgrounds in the park: the one detailed here is the most inviting to tent campers; the other caters to RVs.

Arriving at the west edge of the park on OH 372/Stoney Creek Road, the first of the park's two 15-acre lakes sits on the right. If you're not paying attention you may miss it, as it's situated back in a wooded ravine 40 yards from a paved parking area that also serves a picnic shelter. Stewart Lake is accessible for fishing from its entire perimeter by following the Stewart Lake Trail. Although you will have to carry your canoe or kayak to the lake for some calm paddling, the remote environment is worth the extra effort.

Across the road from the Stewart Lake parking area is a similar paved parking area with a sign welcoming campers to the hike-in-only, 18-site campground. A paved path rolls down a slight grade to the campground and is for foot traffic only. The area sits in the bottom of a

Campsites at Scioto Trail State Park are well laid out and offer plenty of privacy.

KEY INFORMATION

LOCATION: 144 Lake Road
Chillicothe, Ohio 45601

CONTACT: 740-887-4818
(Tar Hollow State Park handles calls),
parks.ohiodnr.gov/sciototrail

OPEN: Year-round; limited facilities in winter;
camp store closed November–April

SITES: 18 hike-in, nonelectric

EACH SITE HAS: Picnic table, fire ring

WHEELCHAIR ACCESS: None

ASSIGNMENT: First come, first served

REGISTRATION: Self-registration station at
campground office, if office closed

AMENITIES: Pit toilets, water fountains, camp
store, sports courts, playground, minigolf,
swimming beach, boat rentals, canoe launch

PARKING: In designated parking area

FEE: $22; deduct $3 in winter

ELEVATION: 829 feet

RESTRICTIONS

PETS: On leash only

QUIET HOURS: 10 p.m.–7 a.m.

FIRES: In fire ring

ALCOHOL: Prohibited in public areas in every
state park but may be consumed within the
confines of a rented cabin, cabin site, lodge
room, or campsite

VEHICLES: 2/site

OTHER: Gathering firewood prohibited;
maximum 6 people/site

small, forested valley with a stream cutting through the middle. The first sites on the right, 56–59, are spread out on a level, mowed lawn area with a few medium-size trees for shade. These four sites do catch some road noise from Stoney Creek Road, which is the primary thoroughfare of the park, but they are perfect for a multiple family camping excursion. Site 60 is the next site on the right and matches the first four in description but sits next to the access path to a second section of the campground.

Where the campground splits into two, single file sections, at site 73, is a bulletin board with information on current events at the park, as well as camp rules. Next to the bulletin board is a water spigot. Across the paved path from the bulletin board are two pit toilets. The path continues up a slight grade to site 69, the last spot in that row. The forest climbs quickly at the rear of site 69, so expect woodland critters to drop down for a nighttime visit—nothing too big and bad, but you'll see an occasional raccoon.

Return to the split in the path and cross the small stream that flows through a culvert to reach the second row of sites. A dozen yards beyond the stream crossing and to the right, in the middle of a 10-yard forest clearing, are sites 61 and 62. During the green season, head-high vegetation grows along the streambed and between the site rows for added privacy. In fall the aroma of the encroaching forest is strong, making it a pleasant time to occupy this campground. Sites 63–68 complete the north row. They are the farthest from the parking area and road (200 yards), so go straight to one of those sites for the most tranquility.

As you enter the hike-in campground pathway, a wide path through the forest will be on the left. This 0.6-mile trail leads uphill to the fire tower and a grand view of the park. Another worthwhile trek is the Church Hollow Trail, which connects to the main RV campground at Caldwell Lake. This 2-mile trail rises over 200 feet in elevation as it explores heavy forest before returning to the main campground. Also check out the old log church at the campground and the history behind it.

Scioto Trail State Park: Hike-In Campground

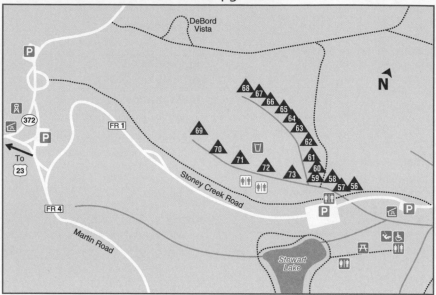

GETTING THERE

From Chillicothe, follow US 23 south 9.5 miles to OH 372 and turn left to enter the park. Travel 1.8 miles to the primitive camping area parking on the left.

GPS COORDINATES: N39° 13.078' W82° 57.722'

40

⛺ Shawnee State Park

Beauty ★★★ Privacy ★★★ Spaciousness ★★ Quiet ★★ Security ★★★ Cleanliness ★★★

First-class hiking trails lead visitors to inspiring views and exploration of more than 63,000 acres of vast forest.

This area is one of the most naturally scenic in the state, with steep hills and cut valleys, which has earned Shawnee State Park and the surrounding state forest the nickname The Little Smokies of Ohio. The mix of hemlock and deciduous forest that shades most of the campground presents a mountain forest atmosphere. The renowned Turkey Creek Nature Center, located 1 mile north of the campground on OH 125, offers programs that are informative and entertaining for all visitors, especially young campers. Call 740-858-6652 for the naturalist's schedule. Walking about in the Shawnee State Park and forest any time of the year is a pleasurable experience, but for a wildflower show, including rare orchids, visit in late spring. The abundant natural diversity on display throughout the park and forest will keep visitors occupied, making a multiday stay a must.

Located on the lower slope of a hill between Turkey Creek Lake and Roosevelt Lake is the campground. The 107 sites are dispersed through the woods and open areas and up and down the slope, creating a variety of site styles at various elevations. The first sites on the

A campfire is a welcome treat on a cool, misty night at Shawnee State Park.

KEY INFORMATION

LOCATION: 4404 OH 125
West Portsmouth, Ohio 45663

CONTACT: 740-858-4561(seasonal),
740-858-6652(park office);
parks.ohiodnr.gov/shawnee

OPEN: Year-round; limited facilities in winter,
but shower house remains open

SITES: 12 nonelectric, 95 electric

EACH SITE HAS: Picnic table, fire ring

WHEELCHAIR ACCESS: No specific
ADA-accessible sites

ASSIGNMENT: Walk-in sites first come, first
served; others may be reserved at 866-644-
6727 or ohiostateparks.reserveamerica.com

REGISTRATION: Self-registration station at
campground office, if office closed

AMENITIES: Showers, flush toilets, laundry,
camp store, sports courts, playground,
swimming beach, boat rentals, minigolf,
nature center, 18-hole golf course,
nature center

PARKING: At each site

FEE: $26 electric, $22 nonelectric;
deduct $3 in winter

ELEVATION: 717 feet

RESTRICTIONS

PETS: On leash only

QUIET HOURS: 10 p.m.–7 a.m.

FIRES: In fire ring, which must not be moved

ALCOHOL: Prohibited in public areas in every
state park but may be consumed within the
confines of a rented cabin, cabin site, lodge
room, or campsite

VEHICLES: 2/site

OTHER: Gathering firewood prohibited;
maximum 6 people/site

---

right past the campground office are 57, 59, 61, and 63, sitting on a shelf 20 feet below the road and parking space and shaded by large trees. They're not bad tent sites, but better ones exist if they are not occupied. The sites at the northern tip of the campground are popular with RV owners, but as the campground road turns back uphill and straightens out, site 99 is on the right. The heart of site 99 is up a small rise and back from the road 10 yards. Across the road are sites 104 and 106, both set on a ledge in a woodlot. Back across the road and up a short lane to the right are three tent-only sites—108, 109, and 110—all are walk-in and can't be reserved.

At the southern turn of the campground's long section are sites 40 and 42. Both have a dozen wooden steps leading up from the parking space to the site, which is tough to see up on the ridge. Site 38 is half as high, with only six steps needed to handle the climb. The forest surrounds each site separately like little barricaded forts, which makes them some of the quietest in the campground. Behind these sites the hill continues to rise 300 feet before reaching the top. There are no trails through this section of the forest, so listen to the undisturbed fauna going about its business after dark for some bedtime entertainment.

The block-shaped section with sites 1–33 is the closest to the campground office and the busiest area of the campground. A minigolf course, an amphitheater, and a playground are the attractions here. Traveling through the 100-yard-wide block of sites, search out site 8 on the uphill corner, as it separates itself from the pack with a few extra yards of space between neighboring sites. Also on the uphill side, but at the next corner, are tent-only sites 12–14. These sites are similar in layout and forest cover to sites 40 and 42. Of the three, site 14 gets the nod for creating a private, forest flora camping experience.

A modern lodge at the park allows campers to use the lodge's swimming pool for a small fee. To find the lodge, take Forest Service Road 16 off OH 125, just north of the headwaters of Turkey Creek Lake. To take a walk through a deep section of the 63,000-acre state forest, jump on the 7.2-mile Shawnee State Forest Day Hike Trail and follow the blue blazes. The trailhead is located on the east side of OH 125, opposite the turn to the Turkey Creek Nature Center. To explore the state forest from the road, try the self-guided auto tour outlined by the Division of Forestry. For a brochure and map, visit ohiodnr.com and follow the Forest links, or call 740-858-6685.

Shawnee State Park

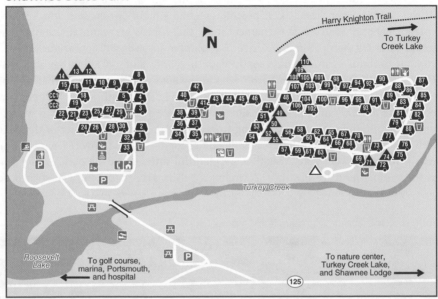

GETTING THERE

From Portsmouth, follow US 52 southwest 6.6 miles to OH 125 and turn right. Travel 5.2 miles to the park entrance on the left.

GPS COORDINATES: N38° 43.657' W83° 10.745'

41

⛺ Stonelick State Park

Beauty ★★ Privacy ★★ Spaciousness ★★★ Quiet ★★ Security ★★★ Cleanliness ★★★

Fossil hunters consider Stonelick a treasure chest of rare finds.

With clear, clean water, 200-acre Stonelick Lake allows electric motors only and begs for recreational use. The sights, sounds, and smells of this gem of a lake rise and mix with the forest that scatters over Stonelick State Park, creating a naturally pleasing atmosphere. If you prefer a shot of man-made excitement, note that Ohio's premium amusement park, Kings Island, is less than a 30-minute drive away. But I'm sure you will appreciate Stonelick's welcoming, peaceful environment to soothe your tired body and soul after a day at the park.

Camping at Stonelick is diverse, from sites at the edge of brushy habitat that supports entertaining birdlife year-round to premium sites along the lakeshore with direct water access. There are only nine premium sites, so be sure to reserve at least two weeks in advance. The grounds are slightly sloping toward the lake, with the center of the campground a fairly even plane. The area is mostly shaded—but not covered with a heavy canopy—from the sweet gum trees that are plentiful throughout the park. At the north tip of the campground are sites 14–17, circling a cul-de-sac. These four well-spaced sites

A brushy shoreline separates campsites from Stonelick Lake here.

KEY INFORMATION

LOCATION: 2895 Lake Drive
Pleasant Plain, Ohio 45162

CONTACT: 513-625-6593(seasonal), 513-734-4323 (East Harbor State Park handles off-season calls); parks.ohiodnr.gov/stonelick

OPEN: Year-round; limited facilities in winter, including sites 1–5, 42–115

SITES: 6 nonelectric, 108 electric

EACH SITE HAS: Picnic table, fire ring

WHEELCHAIR ACCESS: Site 1 is
ADA-accessible

ASSIGNMENT: Walk-in sites first come, first served; others may be reserved at 866-644-6727 or ohiostateparks.reserveamerica.com

REGISTRATION: Self-registration station at campground office, if office closed

AMENITIES: Showers, flush toilets, laundry, camp store, sports courts, playground, swimming beach, boat rentals, bike rentals

PARKING: At each site

FEE: $23 nonelectric, $26 electric;
deduct $3 in winter

ELEVATION: 902 feet

RESTRICTIONS

PETS: On leash only and permitted in sites
7–76 only

QUIET HOURS: 10 p.m.–7 a.m.

FIRES: In fire ring, which must not be moved

ALCOHOL: Prohibited in public areas in every state park but may be consumed within the confines of a rented cabin, cabin site, lodge room, or campsite

VEHICLES: 2/site

OTHER: Gathering firewood prohibited; maximum 6 people/site; no parking on the grass; all bicycles ridden after dark must have proper lighting.

are the most out of the way and are backed by forest and brush. If the lakeshore sites are occupied, consider one of these.

The next cul-de-sac to the south contains four of the premium sites, which are spaced by 10 yards. Sites 24–27 are on the lakeshore, but the shoreline at that point is fairly brushy with limited access to cast a line or shove off in a canoe. On the bright side, the birding there is great. If that circle of sites is filled, try for the neighboring cul-de-sac that also sits at the water's edge with sites 28–30. These sites are almost level with the water, so sliding a kayak in is easy. Actually, next to site 29 is the dirt rental boat launch point. (There's also a boat ramp for canoes and kayaks located off of OH 727, on the west side of the lake.) Site 29 begs for a couple of chairs positioned at the water's edge after dinner, to release any stress and absorb the pleasant effects of a sunset over the lake.

The next cul-de-sac to the south holds the nonelectric sites, 33–39. Of those sites, 34 and 35 offer views of the lake, but no direct access. The spaciousness of those sites—each is about 15 by 15 yards—creates a quiet retreat with a pretty little lake to admire. This section may be the quietest for tent campers because of the abundant space and the brushy screen between the neighboring group of sites.

The main loop of the campground is shaped like a peanut, with two premium sites (53 and 55) sitting at the western edge of the group. Sites 53 and 55 feature lake views, but no water access; a brush-covered, steep slope several yards long keeps campers at bay, but the higher vantage point allows a panoramic view. The center of the peanut is filled with sites that have a neighborhood feel; they're not too close to each other, but each site is open to the next one. Sprouting off the peanut section and ending at a cul-de-sac are sites 68–86. At the outer edge of that cul-de-sac is site 76, which sits above a southern cove of the lake. Note that the lake is only visible from site 76 when the leaves are off. The last and most southern section includes sites 90–113. These are the first sites you'll encounter on the right as you enter the campground and fill the bill of most RVers—they're flat with no low branches to obstruct awnings.

The bedrock that lies under Stonelick was raised near the surface as the Appalachian Mountains were created thousands of years ago. That fact has drawn fossil hunters to the region for centuries. Fossils of the rarest form and variety are still collected today throughout southwestern Ohio, but especially in the region that includes Stonelick State Park. Designated areas are open to fossil collecting. Call the park office at 513-734-4323 to secure permission and the permitted locations.

Stonelick State Park

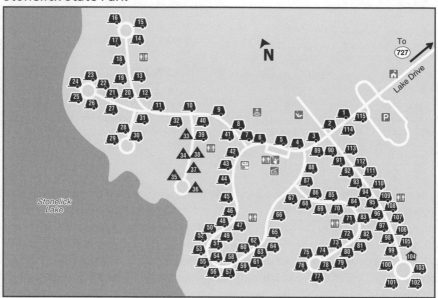

GETTING THERE

From Blanchester, travel 5.8 miles southwest on OH 133 to Edenton. Follow OH 727 southwest for 2.5 miles to Lake Drive and turn left. Travel 2.2 on Lake Drive to the campground entrance.

GPS COORDINATES: N39° 13.024' W84° 03.527'

CENTRAL

Some campsites at Delaware State Park (see page 145) are spacious enough for two tents.

42

⛺ A. W. Marion State Park

Beauty ★★★ Privacy ★★★ Spaciousness ★★★ Quiet ★★★ Security ★★★ Cleanliness ★★★★

Big fun awaits at small, tranquil Hargus Lake.

An accurate example that great things come in small packages is A. W. Marion State Park and its pleasant little lake. The park covers 309 acres, and its main feature, Hargus Lake, takes up half of that space with 145 acres. The park's fertile soils continue to annually produce some of the most vibrantly colored wildflowers in the state. To see the botanical diversity of the park, cinch up your boot strings and set out on the 3.9-mile Hargus Lake Perimeter Trail that passes through the campground. This hiking trail explores the hills and hollows surrounding the lake, but it doesn't prove too stressful for the average hiker.

Hargus Lake is best explored by boat, and the lake allows electric motors only, so there are no wakes to worry about. Boats are available for rent at the small but well-maintained marina on the west shore, across the lake from the campground. There are three small islands and two peninsulas to explore. The lake was drained in the early 1980s and received fish habitat improvements and was restocked. One lap around serene Hargus Lake in a canoe or kayak will leave you wanting another.

Sprawled out on top of a ridge above Hargus Lake is the park's isolated campground. During summer, the lake is hidden from view by the trees, but in autumn, when the leaves

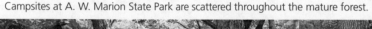

Campsites at A. W. Marion State Park are scattered throughout the mature forest.

KEY INFORMATION

LOCATION: 7317 Warner-Huffer Road
Circleville, Ohio 43113

CONTACT: 740-467-2690 (Buckeye Lake
State Park handles this park's calls),
parks.ohiodnr.gov/awmarion

OPEN: Year-round; walk-in sites only in winter
with limited facilities, including water

SITES: 28 nonelectric, 28 electric

EACH SITE HAS: Fire ring, picnic table

WHEELCHAIR ACCESS: No specific
ADA-accessible sites

ASSIGNMENT: Walk-in sites first come, first
served; others may be reserved at 866-644-
6727 or ohiostateparks.reserveamerica.com

REGISTRATION: Self-registration at
campground entrance

AMENITIES: Pit toilets, playground,
amphitheater, sports courts, boat rentals

PARKING: At each site

FEE: Nonelectric: $22 Apr. 1–Oct. 31,
$19 Nov. 1–Mar. 31; electric: $26 Apr. 1–
Oct. 31, $23 Nov. 1–Mar. 31; $1 less
Sunday–Thursday; $2 more during holidays

ELEVATION: 893 feet

RESTRICTIONS

PETS: On leash only; maximum 2/site

QUIET HOURS: 10 p.m.–7 a.m.

FIRES: In fire ring, which must not be moved

ALCOHOL: Prohibited in public areas in every
state park but may be consumed within the
confines of a rented cabin, cabin site, lodge
room, or campsite

VEHICLES: Must fit on paved pad, maximum
2/site, extra vehicles may be parked in lot
near park office

OTHER: Gathering firewood prohibited;
maximum 6 people/site

fall from the oaks standing throughout the campground, a scenic shot of the lake is revealed from the sites at the western side of the campground. The camping fun begins at the end of a dead-end road. The campground's small size forced planners to squeeze as many sites onto the property as possible. This is apparent if you're trying to find a site where you can spread out. The first sites on the right when entering the campground are the tightest, so drive past those and on around the long loop and watch for site 56 on the right. Site 56 has more elbow room than the previous ones and sports a tent pad and lantern holder as well. Site 57 is similar, and both sit at the edge of a hollow that leads to the lake.

Back near the entrance is a small semiloop with sites 17–27, which also offer a few extra feet to spread out and are a bit deeper and downhill. The Hargus Lake Perimeter Trail passes the edge of site 23, which may bring visitors too close for comfort. Instead, try site 21 for more privacy. Sites 19 and 22 are inside the loop and are good second choices because they are still several yards away from the campground's main road. The last set of sites is in a small loop to the east of the entrance and off by itself. Site 8 offers the most space and rests at the outer edge of the campground.

Stages Pond State Nature Preserve is north of A. W. Marion State Park and worth a visit. Return to Ringold Southern Road and head north to Stout Road. Turn left on Stout and travel to OH 188. Drive southwest on OH 188 and take the first right onto Winchester Road. Go north 2 miles to Hagerty Road and turn left. The nature preserve will be on the right in 2.21 miles. Stages Pond is a kettle lake that you can view from maintained trails. During spring and fall, the lake is a refuge for migrating waterfowl, some of which are rare in Ohio. In summer, the calls and songs of various species of shorebirds echo out across the nature preserve.

A.W. Marion State Park

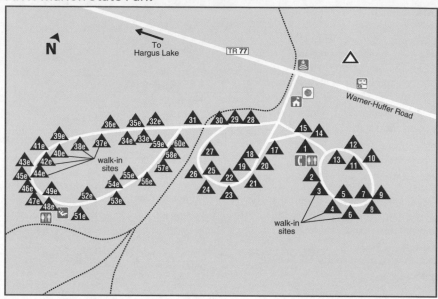

GETTING THERE

From Circleville, follow US 22 east for 3.9 miles to Ringold Southern Road (Township Road 42). Turn left and travel 0.9 mile north to Warner-Huffer Road (TR 77). Turn left and travel west 0.4 mile to the campground entrance on the left.

GPS COORDINATES: N39° 38.073' W82° 52.931'

43

⛺ Delaware State Park

Beauty ★★ Privacy ★★ Spaciousness ★★ Quiet ★★ Security ★★★ Cleanliness ★★★

A lake built to control flooding is now flooded with recreation.

Delaware Lake was constructed by the U.S. Army Corps of Engineers in 1948 for flood control, and it has been a popular recreational destination ever since. The park is less than 30 miles from the state capital. The lake is surrounded by a fair mix of forest and meadows. The mixed forest on the east side of the lake is managed as a wildlife area primarily for hunting, but when hunting season is over, the food plots and other conservational practices are great wildlife-viewing locations. The lake is accessible by designated hiking trails from a few of the campsites, and there are tie-ups for boaters who are willing to leave their boats unattended while hanging out at their site.

The 211 campsites are located along the west side of the lake and split up into four clusters, which look like five-petal flowers with bare stems from a bird's-eye view. Each cluster contains 50 sites, with 10 sites per branch. In the center of each cluster is a shower house with flush toilets and a laundry room. The first right past the campground office and store leads to Area Four and passes the park road (remember the flower stem?) to Area Three on

These boxes at Delaware State Park attract tree swallows, which help control the insect population here.

KEY INFORMATION

LOCATION: 5202 US 23 N
Delaware, Ohio 43015

CONTACT: 740-548-4631,
parks.ohiodnr.gov/delaware

OPEN: Year-round; limited facilities in winter,
including sites 51–100, shower house, water

SITES: 211 electric

EACH SITE HAS: Picnic table, fire ring

WHEELCHAIR ACCESS: Sites 80, 89, 90, and
100, as well as showers and restrooms, are
ADA-accessible

ASSIGNMENT: Walk-in sites first come, first
served; others may be reserved at 866-644-
6727 or ohiostateparks.reserveamerica.com

REGISTRATION: At campground office;
self-register at office if closed

AMENITIES: Showers, flush toilets, laundry,
camp store, game room, boat ramp, boat

rentals, bike rentals, disc-golf course,
swimming beach

PARKING: At each site

FEE: $30; deduct $3 in winter

ELEVATION: 953 feet

RESTRICTIONS

PETS: On leash only

QUIET HOURS: 10 p.m.–7 a.m.

FIRES: In fire ring, which must not be moved

ALCOHOL: Prohibited in public areas in every
state park but may be consumed within the
confines of a rented cabin, cabin site, lodge
room, or campsite

VEHICLES: 2/site; boat trailers count as one

OTHER: Gathering firewood prohibited;
maximum 6 people/site;
maximum 3 tents/site

the way. Note that Area Three can be bypassed for tent camping. These open sites are more attractive to RVers who like the feel of a suburban neighborhood.

Area Four holds sites 1–50. The first branch (or petal) opens with sites 1 and 2, both shaded and with no neighbors across the lane. Sites 12 and 13 sit in the second branch and are set back in a pocket in the wood's edge. The third branch offers site 27, surrounded by a mix of various sizes of deciduous trees. The 1.5-mile Briarpatch Trail, which winds through a young forest, meadows, and a couple of ponds hidden in the woods, passes behind site 27 as well. The 20 sites in the fourth and fifth branches of Area Four are better left for RVs.

Return to the lane you came in on (Park Road 27), turn right, and travel approximately 0.4 mile to Area Two. The first branch consists of sites 101–111. Pass these up and drive into the second branch to site 113 on the right, a shaded spot not far from the shower house and bathroom, yet far enough to enjoy some peaceful camping. The third branch has dandy site 128, with views of the lake. From this site, you can also access the Big Foot Trail, which passes between the site and the shoreline en route to the Fisherman's Trail that heads to a quiet lake cove.

If popular site 128 is taken, slide up the fourth branch that includes sites 134–145. All 10 offer camping under large maple trees, and the sites are staggered to reduce the curious neighbor syndrome. Up the fifth branch, sites 155 and 156 are the best, also with a staggered position and a thick vegetation screen between them.

Leave Area Two and drive north on Park Road 27 for approximately 0.75 mile to Area One. It's the farthest from the campground entrance, which weeds out most RVers, and is home to two of the best branches of the campground. Area One also has the most dense forest surrounding and jetting out into the campsites. The first branch has sites 158–166. Site 160 spreads out under a mature oak. Site 163 is deep and nestled in a group of young trees. The second branch features site 180, a wider site for a couple of tents. Skip the third branch with sites 181–191, unless you prefer wide-open yard camping. The fourth branch extends toward the lake, which is only a short walk through the forest. The forest borders sites 195 and 196, and site 197 completes the trifecta, with all three just steps away from a trail leading to a set of boat tie-ups.

The meadows throughout the park contain bird boxes attached to skinny posts. What may appear to be the result of a bird box–building contest is actually a well-conceived and well-managed insect control plan. The boxes, which are placed in a grid 25 feet apart, attract breeding tree swallows. These insect-eating machines swoop over the open wetlands and marshes, catching flies and mosquitoes to feed their young. An adult tree swallow feeds its babies 6,000 insects per day, so this is an impressively efficient insect-control system.

If you're looking for a nearby day trip, check out Olentangy Indian Caverns. Just 7 miles south of the town of Delaware (on busy US 23 and then right on Home Road), the caverns are open April–October. For less than $10 you will be guided into the underground realm of caves that were once an important asset for the Delaware Indians.

Delaware State Park

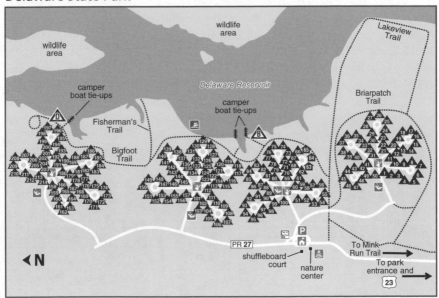

GETTING THERE

From Delaware, travel north on US 23 for 5.5 miles to the park entrance on the right. Follow signage to the campground.

GPS COORDINATES: N40° 22.676' W83° 04.418'

44

⚑ Dillon State Park

Beauty ★★ Privacy ★ Spaciousness ★★ Quiet ★★ Security ★★★★ Cleanliness ★★★

Camping at Dillon State Park puts you right in between Zanesville and Newark, which both offer plenty of natural and cultural history to explore.

Remaining evidence of the progression of transportation in America can be seen nowhere better than in and within a few miles of Dillon State Park. The 2,285-acre state park is cut in half by the Licking River (still a favorite of avid canoeists), which was a primary travel route for American Indians that led to the larger Muskingum River running through downtown Zanesville. Today, the Licking River is paused by the Dillon Dam (built in 1961) for flood control. At Blackhand Gorge State Nature Preserve, just 8 miles northeast of the park outside Toboso, you will see remnants of the Ohio & Erie Canal system. Canal towpaths and locks are visible from a 4-mile paved trail that follows the Licking River through the pristine gorge. Spending a few minutes perched atop the steep riverbank offers a peaceful break to soak up the smell of the river, the sights of sandstone cliffs, and the sounds of birds singing and flittering about the tree canopy. The interurban railroad connected Zanesville to Newark and Columbus by following the Licking River through the Dillon region, as well as the Blackhand Gorge. Passing through nearby Zanesville is the Old National Road, which crosses the Y-Bridge—a unique and historic bridge, built in the shape its name implies, that spans the confluence of the Licking and Muskingum Rivers. So don't be alarmed if you ask

In late autumn, you'll have your pick of sites at Dillon State Park.

KEY INFORMATION

LOCATION: 5265 Dillon Hills Dr.
Nashport, Ohio 43830-9568

CONTACT: 740-453-4377,
parks.ohiodnr.gov/dillon

OPEN: Year-round; heated showers closed
December–March

SITES: 183 electric, 12 nonelectric,
20 walk-in equestrian sites

EACH SITE HAS: Picnic table, fire ring

WHEELCHAIR ACCESS: Restrooms are
accessible, but no specific sites.

ASSIGNMENT: Walk-in sites first come, first
served; others may be reserved at 866-644-
6727 or ohiostateparks.reserveamerica.com

REGISTRATION: At camp office; self-
registration station on front of camp office

AMENITIES: Camp store, showers, flush toilets,
laundry, pay phone, playground, sports
courts, nature center, marina, boat ramp,
archery range, disc-golf course; free Wi-Fi

available at camp store for registered
campers

PARKING: At each site, except tent-only sites
have a parking area

FEE: $28 electric, $22 nonelectric;
deduct $3 in winter

ELEVATION: 945 feet

RESTRICTIONS

PETS: On leash only

QUIET HOURS: 10 p.m.–7 a.m.

FIRES: In fire ring, which must not be moved

ALCOHOL: Prohibited in public areas in every
state park but may be consumed within the
confines of a rented cabin, cabin site, lodge
room, or campsite

VEHICLES: 2/site if tent camping;
1/site if RV camping

OTHER: Gathering firewood prohibited;
14-day stay limit; maximum 6 people/site;
parking on grass prohibited; major supplies
available in Zanesville

for directions from a local resident and they tell you to take a right or left in the middle of the bridge. The Muskingum River was a major steamboat route that delivered supplies for the growing settlements in east-central Ohio.

While camping at Dillon State Park, watch for members of the abundant deer population that live in the park—they don't hesitate to form groups near the park roads. After passing the campground check station, take a right at the intersection and pass the shower house sitting on the hill on the left. As you reach the left bend in the road, the 12 tent sites (184–195) are on the rise to your left, and their parking area is on both sides of the road. The mowed hill on the right is the sledding hill. You must walk slightly uphill from the parking area, but a mulch pathway keeps it from being muddy on rainy days. The sites are spread evenly throughout a woodlot that is surrounded on three sides by the campground road as it winds its way onward to the electric sites that regularly host RVers. The security at Dillon is top-notch, and the speed limit is sternly enforced, which means that even though the campground road passes by the tent area, drivers travel in a quiet, slow manner.

The woodlot slopes slightly toward the parking area, but this doesn't pose a problem for pitching your tent. Site 189 is the farthest from the parking area and adjoining sites, making it the best spot in this campground. A backdrop of brush curtains off any commotion coming from the RV sites over the ridge. All of the tent sites have a view (sites 185–189 have the best) of the sledding hill that is also a wildlife-viewing area flanked by forest on both sides. Speaking of wildlife, keep your snacks off the picnic table, as the healthy population of squirrels will sneak your treats when your back is turned. To reach the restroom, walk about 20 yards across the campground road. The primary sites are busy through the summer with RVs full of families, but those sites are plenty spacious for big tenting excursions as well.

The Dillon region attracts sportsmen during the hunting seasons because of the expansive wildlife area that joins Dillon State Park's northern boundary and flanks the southbound-flowing Licking River. The Dillon Sportsman Center (dillonsportsmancenter.com) offers a 100-yard rifle range and a 25-yard pistol range and is located on Pleasant Valley Road. To reach it, drive 5.48 miles north on OH 146 from the intersection of OH 146 and Clay Littick Drive and look for the area on the left. Back at the state park, an archery range is located at the bottom of the sledding hill. Sanctioned mountain bike races are held at Dillon State Park's 18-mile bike course, said to be one of the most challenging in the state. And 1,560-acre Dillon Lake is available for unlimited-horsepower boating.

Dillon State Park

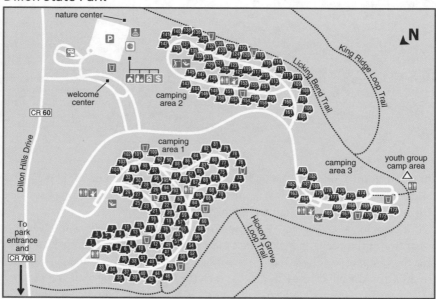

GETTING THERE

From I-70, take Exit 153 in Zanesville and go north on Blue Avenue 0.4 mile to OH 146. Turn left and travel 7.5 miles to County Road 708 (Clay Littick Drive). Turn left and follow CR 708 for 1.5 miles to the campground entrance on the right.

GPS COORDINATES: N40° 00.643' W82° 06.257'

45

Kokosing Lake Campground

Beauty ★★★ Privacy ★★★ Spaciousness ★★★ Quiet ★★ Security ★★★ Cleanliness ★★★

The lake is the star of a Kokosing camping experience, and it will definitely hold your attention.

As you arrive at Kokosing Lake Campground, you may experience flyovers from the many waterfowl species that visit the lake—either migrating or year-round residents. The 185-acre lake is not expansive in size or depth, but it's big in the natural habitat that surrounds it and its fine campground. The U.S. Army Corps of Engineers constructed the Kokosing Dam in 1972 for flood control, and the dammed water is now home to several species of game fish and wildlife that inhabit the surrounding Kokosing Wildlife Area. Kayaking or canoeing from the campground across the lake to the northeast leads to an island shaped like an ice-cream cone and covered with brush. Between this island and the lake's shoreline on the other side of the island, farthest from the campground, is a quiet and hidden portion of the lake that should be the first stop for paddlers with cameras. Slowly paddling around the island, allowing the kayak to simply glide with momentum every other stroke, will allow you to approach the wildlife standing at the water's edge. If a watercraft is not on

Dip your toes in Kokosing Lake from campsites that border the water's edge.

KEY INFORMATION

LOCATION: 18350 Waterford Road Fredericktown, Ohio 43019

CONTACT: Operated by Fredericktown Recreation District: 740-694-1900 (camp office in season), 740-694-8366 (off-season); kokosingcampground.com

OPEN: April 1–October 31

SITES: 48

EACH SITE HAS: Picnic table, fire ring

WHEELCHAIR ACCESS: No specific ADA-accessible sites

ASSIGNMENT: Call 740-694-1900 or visit camp office for reservations; first come, first served for any site not reserved

REGISTRATION: At camp office at campground entrance

AMENITIES: Showers, flush and pit toilets, drinking water, playground, direct access to lake, boat ramp

PARKING: At each site, except for tent sites

FEE: $30 nonelectric, $35 electric

ELEVATION: 1,136 feet

RESTRICTIONS

PETS: On leash only

QUIET HOURS: 11 p.m.–7 a.m.

FIRES: In fire ring

ALCOHOL: Do not publicly consume or display

VEHICLES: 1/site

OTHER: You must be age 18 or older to register for a site; ice and bait available at camp store in season

---

your packing list, don't fret, as most of the lake can be explored with a high-quality pair of binoculars or telephoto camera lens.

The small campground here is well maintained and managed. Although RVs are common in the primary sector, about half of those sites are rented by seasonal campers, so a tranquil lakeside camping mood still exists there. Of the 48 sites, 17 of them—including the four tent sites—are on the lake's edge with great views of the sunrise over the water. After entering the campground, follow the lane straight ahead and pass the restroom on the left, which also has a drinking water spigot and water fountain in front of it, to find the tent sites (43–46). You must walk to these four sites, but inquire with the camp office about tent site designated parking. Site 43 will be partially shaded in the morning hours but in full sun the rest of the day. The other three tent sites receive full sun all day, but access to the lake is only a few steps away. Camping in the tent section is like setting up camp in a wide, nicely mowed backyard, except this yard has a lake adjacent. The shoreline is gravel, which is easy on the feet if a few minutes of wading are needed to cool off. A second drinking water spigot is located in the center of the loop surrounded by sites near the tent section. These loop sites are shaded at least half the day and sit off the water but close enough to see the lake.

Back in the campground's primary section, four lakeside sites are attractive for any camper. Site 15 is shaded nearly all day and offers plenty of space. Site 18 offers the most privacy and has an inlet off the lake, separating it from site 20, which is also shady and quite spacey. But Site 22 gets the nod for the best of this group. It has a large, level area to accommodate large tents and shares occupancy with a shade-giving sycamore. The site is out on a point in the lake, and good fishing can be had not far from shore, as the water depth drops off quickly to the east. After a hot summer day of paddling, fishing, or simply lying around basking in the sun, you'll likely appreciate a shower. Fortunately, a modern shower house is positioned on a hill above the campground, an easy stroll from all sites.

A hiking trail through the woods next to the campground gives hikers a half mile to stretch their legs. Less than a half mile back on Waterford Road is access to the Kokosing Dam. A parking area and bulletin board are available for visitors at the end of a short dam access road. Hikers often use this parking area for day hiking the Kokosing Wildlife Area, which is a mix of forest and fields. The fields are managed as food sources for wildlife, and after several minutes hiking through them, you will discover you are not alone. Depending on the season, pause occasionally and see how many different subspecies of butterflies you can count. Or sit high on the dam and take in the lake view below, where you'll regularly spot pairs of nesting eagles, ospreys, and great egrets.

Kokosing Lake Campground

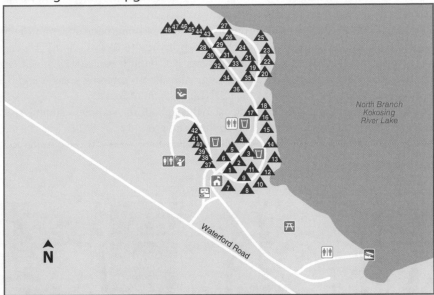

GETTING THERE

From OH 13 northwest of Fredericktown, go west on County Road 6 (Waterford Road) 1.8 miles to the campground entrance on the right.

GPS COORDINATES: N40° 30.379' W82° 35.173'

46

⛺ Mohican State Park and Forest

Beauty ★★★★ Privacy ★★★ Spaciousness ★★★ Quiet ★★★ Security ★★ Cleanliness ★★

A gorge, rich forest, clear river, and campsites are all here to enjoy.

The beauty of the Clear Fork Gorge and the recreational pursuits this area, the geographical star of Ohio, provides make Mohican State Park and Forest one of the state's most visited locations. The state park flanks the Clear Fork Branch of the Mohican River, which flows through the belly of the forest-covered gorge, and the state forest encompasses the 1,110-acre park with nearly 5,000 acres of woodland bliss. A designated gorge overlook allows visitors a bird's-eye view of the forest and river wonderland.

The Mohican State Park and Forest region hosts three campground systems. The most popular is the Class A Campground, which caters primarily to RVs. A short drive deeper into the park will take you to the primitive Class B Campground, aka Hemlock Grove Campground. Located on the north central ridge, above both camping areas A and B, are three park-and-pack sites managed by the ODNR's Division of Forestry.

The Class A Campground is a bustling place throughout the summer camping season. Families preferring the comforts of RVs fill up this campground and create a friendly neighborhood atmosphere. But tucked away in the southwest corner of this busy campground

A short hike leads to this backcountry site at Mohican State Forest.

KEY INFORMATION

LOCATION: 3116 OH 3
Loudonville, Ohio 44842

CONTACT: 419-994-5125; parks.ohiodnr.gov
/mohican(campgrounds in park), forestry.
ohiodnr.gov/mohican (park-and-pack sites)

OPEN: Year-round; limited facilities in winter,
but shower house in Class A area open

SITES: 35 nonelectric, 151 electric

EACH SITE HAS: Picnic table, fire ring;
park-and-pack sites have only fire ring

WHEELCHAIR ACCESS: Site 112 in Class A
campground and shower house are
ADA-accessible.

ASSIGNMENT: Class A sites may be
reserved at 866-644-6727 or
ohiostateparks.reserveamerica.com;
Class B and state forest park-and-pack sites
are first come, first served.

REGISTRATION: At campground office;
self-register at office if closed

AMENITIES: Showers, flush and pit toilets,
laundry, pay phone, swimming pool,
playground, sports courts, canoe launch,
commissary, nature center

PARKING: At each site

FEE: $32 electric, $24 nonelectric; deduct $3 in
winter; state forest park-and-pack sites are
free, but must self-register

ELEVATION: 928 feet

RESTRICTIONS

PETS: On leash only

QUIET HOURS: 10 p.m.–7 a.m.

FIRES: In fire ring

ALCOHOL: Prohibited in public areas in every
state park but may be consumed within the
confines of a rented cabin, cabin site, lodge
room, or campsite; prohibited in state forest
park-and-pack sites

VEHICLES: 2/site; no parking on grass

OTHER: Gathering firewood prohibited;
visitors must pay entry fee;
maximum 6 people/site

---

are 10 nonelectric sites that can only be accessed by foot. After passing through the main campground gate and registration station, take the first left and on the left is the parking area for the walk-in sites. Across from this parking area is a restroom, and a few steps to the left of the restroom is a potable water source.

From the parking area, cross the short footbridge over a drainage ditch to find sites 1–4 spread from left to right. These four sites sit just 40 yards from the river on mowed cutouts among a mix of short ornamental shrubs and smaller deciduous trees, so there's plenty of shade. The preferred sites of this group are 5–10, which sit only a few steps from the water. These riverside sites are normally full during summer weekends, but springtime paddlers and autumn foliage fans will find ample vacancy. Large sycamores intermixed with additional tall trees provide cool camping along the river. Site 10 receives the least amount of passing foot traffic.

The Class B Campground entrance is near one of the Mohican region's most visited landmarks—a covered bridge over the Clear Fork River. To access the campground, you must drive through Hemlock Grove Picnic Area, just east of the bridge. A self-registration kiosk welcomes campers to the 25-site, nonelectric campground. The campground road follows the river, with all sites on the opposite side of the road's edge. Potable water and pit toilets are available across from site 18, as is fishing access and parking. The trout fishing here is considered as good as it gets in Ohio. During early and late seasons, the campsites are regularly used by anglers. The last site on the dead-end road, site 25, provides the most privacy. The Hemlock Gorge hiking trail connects the Class B Area to the Class A Area and provides a pleasing stroll along one of Ohio's most scenic rivers. Keep in mind that this stretch of river gets a steady stream of autos touring the gorge, especially on weekends, so expect to deal with sightseers near the covered bridge.

For campers who want a deep-woods experience without neighbors, the Mohican State Forest's park-and-pack sites provide the fix. Ten of these remote campsites are scattered throughout the Mohican State Forest. Sites 1–7 cater to equestrians along popular bridle trails. Sites 8, 9, and 10 are situated on Hickory Ridge, which runs along the north-central border of the Mohican State Forest. With access to these three sites by mountain bike or on foot only, they are premium tent-camping targets (a fire ring is the only item provided). A gravel road leads to a small parking area (patrolled by law enforcement), with signage that points the way to each site. Site 8 is a 10-minute casual walk from the parking area (even with a pack of gear). Keep watch for the occasional fast-moving mountain biker, as the multiuse trail is a favorite with cyclists. Site 8 is similar to 9 and 10—laid out on a heavily forested finger ridge, near the rim of the river gorge—but it offers the least amount of space and not much of a view. Site 9 is less crowded, with smaller trees and ground brush, but it is a 15-minute walk from the car. Site 10 requires the longest trek, 20 minutes, but it's worth the extra effort for the remote experience. These sites lead campers through rich forests that host seldom-seen flora and fauna, such as the wild blue phlox that blooms in spring.

GETTING THERE

From Loudonville, take OH 3 south 2.3 miles to the Mohican State Park entrance. Class A Area camping is on right through the main entrance. To reach the Class B Area, continue on OH 3 past the main entrance 0.2 mile to OH 97 and turn right. Follow OH 97 for 3 miles to a park road (signage posted) and turn right. Follow this road 1.25 miles to the campground across the covered bridge and to the right. For Mohican State Forest camping, from the covered bridge, continue on the park road 1 mile to County Road 939. Travel north 0.6 mile to CR 3006, turn right, and go 0.2 mile to Township Road 3006. Follow TR 3006 for 0.9 mile to the small parking area on the right, at the end of the dead-end road.

GPS COORDINATES:
Class A Area: N40° 36.580' W82° 15.450'
Class B Area: N40° 36.819' W82° 18.983'
State Forest Sites 8–10: N40° 37.216' W82° 17.109'

Mohican State Park and Forest

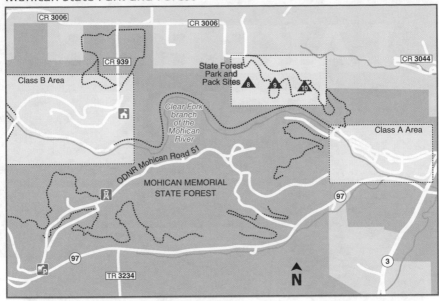

Mohican State Park and Forest Class B Area Campground

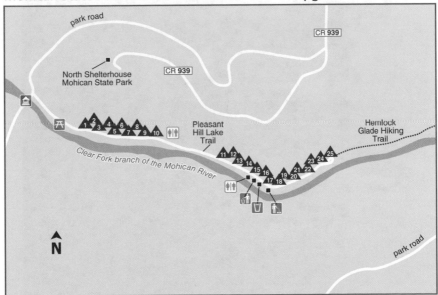

LAKE ERIE REGION

Adventurous campers can set up at the cliff's edge at South Bass Island State Park (see page 168).

47

⚠ East Harbor State Park

Beauty ★★ Privacy ★★ Spaciousness ★★ Quiet ★★ Security ★★★★ Cleanliness ★★★

A day spent walking among Lake Erie's amazing natural resources is one you will long remember.

The shores of western Lake Erie continue to be a popular vacation destination. This is true for families and adventurous individuals alike. Seven million people visit the great lake each year, but there are still quiet places to take in the abundance of natural beauty. East Harbor State Park is one of those places. Situated on the east side of the Catawba peninsula, and on the western shore of East Harbor, the park is surrounded by vacation activities such as fishing, wildlife-watching, and sightseeing. Inside the park is the Ohio State Park System's largest campground. Even so, tent campers have their place where RVs don't tread (though they are within sight).

Campground sections B, C, and E cater to RVs of every size. A few tents are regularly sprinkled among them, but for serious tent campers, sections A and D (G is a group section) are quietly positioned in forested settings. Section A is the largest of the tent sections and surrounds a wide-open playing field and playground area. Sites A1–A89 line both sides of several paved roads that create a gridlike layout. Sites A90–A114 line the outer perimeter of section A, which means the rear of each site is shaded, and some of these sites have total

This path leads to excellent fishing at East Harbor State Park.

KEY INFORMATION

LOCATION: 1169 N. Buck Road
Lakeside-Marblehead, Ohio 43440-9610

CONTACT: 419-734-5857,
parks.ohiodnr.gov/eastharbor

OPEN: Year-round; in winter only sites B1–B40
and A1–A12 are open, with water at check-
in office

SITES: 160 nonelectric, 352 electric

EACH SITE HAS: Picnic table, fire ring

WHEELCHAIR ACCESS: Restrooms are
ADA-accessible, but no specific sites

ASSIGNMENT: Walk-in sites first come, first
served; others may be reserved at 866-644-
6727 or ohiostateparks.reserveamerica.com

REGISTRATION: At entrance station;
check in after 3 p.m., check out at 1 p.m.

AMENITIES: Showers, flush toilets, laundry,
camp store, game room, boat ramp,
fish-cleaning station, bike rentals, disc-golf
course, swimming beach, archery range,
Wi-Fi access at camp store (fee)

PARKING: At each site

FEE: $28 nonelectric, $36 electric

ELEVATION: 586 feet

RESTRICTIONS

PETS: On leash only

QUIET HOURS: 10 p.m.–7 a.m.

FIRES: In fire ring, which must not be moved

ALCOHOL: Prohibited in public areas in every
state park but may be consumed within the
confines of a rented cabin, cabin site, lodge
room, or campsite

VEHICLES: 2/site

OTHER: Gathering firewood prohibited;
maximum 6 people/site

---

shade. Sites A116–A140 are in full shade, while sites A141–A179 are open to the sun. Sites A79–A89 are at the back side of section A and the most quiet sites away from other section A campers and campground traffic rolling in and out of sections B and A.

Section D, located on the opposite side of the campground from section A, is tucked away in a small wooded grove and has 20 sites. Sites D1–D16 are comfortable for tent campers and provide efficient tent-pitching space. Situated away from the main campground road, section D is quiet and peaceful. A short walk from section D is evidence of the last glacial period. Glacial grooves were left behind in exposed rock by the glaciers' last retreat. The grooves are open for campers to walk on and touch.

The harbors are protected from Lake Erie's waves, offering calm waters for paddlers. Bring your camera on your paddling adventure, and chances are high that you will find plenty of waterfowl to photograph. The rocks protecting the harbor shoreline host a variety of wildlife for viewing or photographing. Snakes are plentiful and regularly expose themselves on the rocks before or after feeding on baitfish and frogs. During the three primary camping seasons, East Harbor State Park hosts several conservational programs for campers to participate in, some of which provide an in-depth look into the wildlife that thrives there. East Harbor State Park is a boater's ideal base camp. A large parking area near the registration station is available for tent campers who need a place to park their boat trailers overnight.

East Harbor's hiking trails lead visitors through the lakeshore's diverse habitats. It's wise to bring a bird identification guidebook with you on your hike, as the area is host to hundreds of species, some that stay year-round and others just resting as they journey through.

This region of Lake Erie is rich with sightseeing opportunities. A historic lighthouse sits at the tip of Marblehead Peninsula, skirted by a rocky shoreline. The waves continue to work on those rocks, exhibiting a great show of nature's power. Several wineries feature some of the finest wine-making grapes in the world, which grow well in the rich soil near Lake Erie. Back at the state park, a 1,500-foot sand beach awaits swimmers. Looking out from Lake Erie's shore, you'll see islands on the horizon, and a ferry system carries visitors to those islands daily.

East Harbor State Park

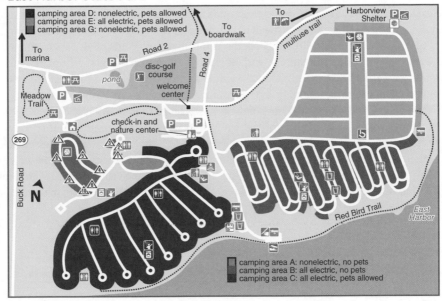

GETTING THERE

From OH 2 on the north shore of Sandusky Bay, take OH 269 north 2.3 miles to OH 163. Go east on OH 163 for 0.4 mile to OH 269 and turn left. Go north 1 mile to the campground entrance on the right.

GPS COORDINATES: N41° 32.689' W82° 49.226'

48

⚤ Geneva State Park

Beauty ★★ Privacy ★★ Spaciousness ★★ Quiet ★★ Security ★★★ Cleanliness ★★★

This summertime resort offers both man-made fun and natural attractions.

The eastern basin of Lake Erie draws thousands of anglers and boaters from several states away. Record-size walleye and steelhead trout are treasures caught regularly here. The water rushing over a mix of rock and sandy shores also brings thousands of visitors to simply sit and watch the Great Lake breathe in and out. Geneva State Park offers visitors more to do than they can accomplish in only a few days, so plan to camp here and make an interesting trip even more exciting. Camping out with numerous species of birds that frequent the shoreline habitat keeps bird-watchers flipping the pages of their identification books.

A 2-mile paved path runs from the camp entrance to the summer resort town of Geneva-on-the-Lake, east of the park. The summer hot spot offers waterslides, arcades, and other beach town entertainment. The climate and soil of this region are conducive to growing grapes, so dozens of vineyards dot the area and welcome visitors to taste the results of their harvests. A glass of locally made wine with a few fresh walleye fillets make a dandy camp dinner.

Spend the evening along Lake Erie at Geneva State Park.

KEY INFORMATION

LOCATION: 4499 Padanarum Road
Geneva, Ohio 44041

CONTACT: 440-466-8400,440-466-7565
(marina); parks.ohiodnr.gov/geneva

OPEN: Year-round; limited amenities and only
sites 38–93 open in winter

SITES: 89 electric,7 nonelectric

EACH SITE HAS: Picnic table, fire ring

WHEELCHAIR ACCESS: No specific
ADA-accessible sites

ASSIGNMENT: Walk-in sites first come, first
served; others may be reserved at 866-644-
6727 or ohiostateparks.reserveamerica.com

REGISTRATION: At campground office;
self-register at office if closed

AMENITIES: Showers, flush toilets, laundry,
camp store, marina, boat ramp, swimming
beach, fish-cleaning station, sports courts,
archery range

PARKING: At each site, single file on pad;
overflow parking in north visitors lot

FEE: $30 electric, $26 nonelectric;
deduct $3 in winter

ELEVATION: 582 feet

RESTRICTIONS

PETS: On leash only

QUIET HOURS: 10 p.m.–7 a.m.

FIRES: In fire ring, which must not be moved

ALCOHOL: Prohibited in public areas in every
state park but may be consumed within the
confines of a rented cabin, cabin site, lodge
room, or campsite

VEHICLES: 2/site; no tow vehicles permitted on
grass, but boat trailers may be on grass

OTHER: Gathering firewood prohibited; maximum 6 people/site; visitors permitted until
10 p.m.; juvenile campers must provide written permission from parents to camp alone.

Tucked back in a woodlot, 700 feet from the Lake Erie shore, is Geneva State Park's campground. Most campers who stay at this campground are either boating or fishing Lake Erie or enjoying some other Lake Erie adventure. The swimming beach is only a 0.25-mile walk from the campground entrance. After passing through the gate at the campground office, overflow camping is offered in the form of seven sites on an open lawn. This is not the most aesthetically pleasing spot to pitch a tent, but during the busy boating season running from spring through early fall, the spots come in handy. If you do bring your boat, there's a six-lane boat ramp at the marina, which is just outside the campground. Concessions at the marina offer bait and boating supplies.

Sites 1–37 form a loop that is popular with RVers during the summer season. Small trees are interspersed sparsely in this loop, offering little relief from the summer sun. Tent campers will prefer sites 38 and 40 back on the main campground road and south of the 1–37 section. Those two sites sit at the beginning of the campground's second section and are well spaced with tent-setting spots near the rear of the site for privacy. The campground contour is nearly flat, which means that on rainy days water pools at several of the sites in the 38–93 loop. A spur off that loop holds sites that sit a couple of feet higher than the wetlands surrounding the campground. At the end of this spur is site 68, which drains well even with ample shade.

The insects come out at night along the big lake's brushy flora, so be prepared to fend off mosquitoes. Insect repellent is a must, and a screened dining canopy is a good idea too. The vegetation near the beach area includes a few species that are rare to Ohio, such as beach pea and sea rocket, both Atlantic coast natives. During winter, cross-country skiing and snow-shoeing are popular activities here, and ski and snowshoe rentals are available at the lodge.

Geneva State Park

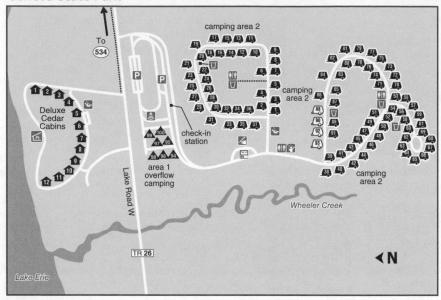

GETTING THERE

From I-90 south of Geneva, take Exit 218 and follow OH 534 north 5.4 miles to the park entrance on the left. Follow the park road 1.8 miles to the campground entrance on the left.

GPS COORDINATES: N41° 51.248' W80° 59.146'

49

⛺ Kelleys Island State Park

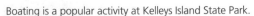

Beauty ★★★ Privacy ★★ Spaciousness ★★ Quiet ★★ Security ★★★ Cleanliness ★★★

The glacial grooves here are a must-see, as there is no other display like them in the world.

Kelleys Island is the most pleasant, quiet, and naturally blessed land mass in Lake Erie. The island hosts the North Pond State Nature Preserve, a 30-acre sanctuary that adjoins the campground's south boundary. The preserve is accessible by a boardwalk and hiking trails, and also features a viewing tower. The star natural attractions of Kelleys Island are the glacial grooves left from the latest glacial period. At 400 feet long, 10 feet deep, and 35 feet wide, the grooves are impressive. Visitors can view all sides of the glacier's footprint from a surrounding walkway with several interpretive stations along the self-guided tour.

Obviously, angling is a popular activity on and around the island. Campers have access to public fishing, and many fishing charters offer their services to visitors who want to catch a few of the infamous Lake Erie walleye. The Kelleys Island Ferry Boat Line (419-798-9763, kelleysislandferry.com) is located in Marblehead and provides year-round service, weather permitting.

When thinking of camping on an island, it's amusing to recall Robinson Crusoe's story of island survival. Camping on Kelleys Island, however, evokes much more pleasant thoughts after walking the gravel shoreline, inspecting the ancient stones, and pondering their story

Boating is a popular activity at Kelleys Island State Park.

KEY INFORMATION

LOCATION: 920 Division St.
Kelleys Island, Ohio 43438

CONTACT: 419-746-2546,
parks.ohiodnr.gov/kelleysisland

OPEN: Year-round, with limited facilities
in winter

SITES: 43 nonelectric, 81 electric

EACH SITE HAS: Picnic table, fire ring

WHEELCHAIR ACCESS: No specific
ADA-accessible sites

ASSIGNMENT: Walk-in sites first come, first
served; others may be reserved at 866-644-
6727 or ohiostateparks.reserveamerica.com

REGISTRATION: At campground office;
self-register at office if closed

AMENITIES: Showers, flush toilets, camp
store, game room, boat ramp, fish-cleaning
station, swimming beach, volleyball court,
kayak rentals

PARKING: At each site

FEE: $32 lakefront, $28 nonelectric

ELEVATION: 592 feet

RESTRICTIONS

PETS: On leash and only at sites 59–76

QUIET HOURS: 10 p.m.–7 a.m.

FIRES: In fire ring

ALCOHOL: Prohibited in public areas in every
state park but may be consumed within the
confines of a rented cabin, cabin site, lodge
room, or campsite

VEHICLES: 1/site

OTHER: No mopeds or golf carts permitted
in campground; gathering firewood prohibited; maximum 6 people/site; limit 2 tents/
site; 14-day stay maximum

that extends over thousands of years. The campground offers amenities that old Robinson would have appreciated, such as a shower and a flush toilet.

Sitting only several yards from and higher than the lake's edge are 10 tent-only sites apart from the main campground circuit. Take a left after passing the campground office to find the short, horseshoe-shaped lane accessing those sites. The first four sites are void of trees, which are missed after playing under the sun all day. The remainder of the tent-only section is interlaced in a young woodlot. Sites 117 and 119 are outside the horseshoe but close to Division Street. In summer the regular buzz of golf carts scooting up and down the street will disturb that nap you hoped to take. Sites 124 and 127 are the following two sites on the lane and contain island yurts—round-sided, wood-frame structures covered with canvas and situated on a wooden deck serving as the floor. Those are the best four sites in the campground for tent camping, and they come with a view of the beach. Site 128 is the last site on the lane that sits between the lane and Lake Erie. It's a long site, nearly 20 yards from the parking pad to the water's edge, and is decorated with 3-foot limestone boulders for erosion control—they also provide crevices for hiding harmless water snakes.

Nine sites line the waterfront, with site 104 being the most spacious for large tents. Shade is sporadic among these lakefront sites, but the refreshing lake breeze is nearly con-stant. Park yourself in a camping chair at site 97 at daybreak, and you'll be treated to a sun-rise show only found on an island. Across the lane is site 94; it's not a waterfront site but has the view of one, and the main shower house is only a few yards away. After site 97, there are seven more waterfront sites before the lane turns inland to the heart of the campground. The last waterfront site is 85, and next to it is a lane that leads to a fish-cleaning shed that is open to all campers.

The campground's interior sites are split into three groups. Sites 1–34 are laid out on both sides of a branch paralleling Division Street, with only a sparse row of trees between them and the road. A shorter branch between that lane and Lake Erie, but similar in shape, hold sites 35–58. All of the sites on those two branches offer lawn camping, with some stray shade from the occasional tree. Sites 59–71 line a lane between the two branches and the lake and are a bit more isolated.

To the northwest of the campground is another state nature preserve, the North Shore Alvar. Alvars are horizontal exposures of limestone exposed by glaciers that are kept open by environmental forces such as wind and the waves working over Kelleys Island's north shoreline. The formations support rare and endangered species of plants such as the northern bog violet. To have a look at this special place, go past the Glacial Grooves State Memorial until the road dead-ends at the boaters' parking area. Enter the preserve on the state park trail to the northwest.

Kelleys Island State Park

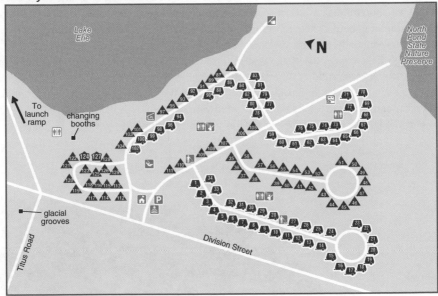

GETTING THERE

From Marblehead, board the Kelleys Island Ferry from 510 West Main Street. From the ferry dock on the southern point of Kelleys Island, go west on East Lake Shore Road 0.3 mile to Division Street and turn right. Follow Division Street 1.4 miles to the campground entrance on the right.

GPS COORDINATES: N41° 36.874' W82° 42.385'

50

⚠ South Bass Island State Park

Beauty ★★★★ Privacy ★★ Spaciousness ★★ Quiet ★★ Security ★★★ Cleanliness ★★★

Enjoy grandstand views of gorgeous Lake Erie from clifftop campsites.

The Victory Hotel, which was located on the property that is now the South Bass Island State Park campground, was destroyed by fire in 1919 but is still a reminder of how long the island has been attracting vacationers. The island's biggest attraction is Put-in-Bay, a tourist hot spot for dining, wine-tasting, nightlife, shopping, and sightseeing, but mostly for night-life. This lively point at the northern tip of the island gets pretty ornery with partiers after dark, so for a laid-back experience, return to the campground as the sun sets.

On the east side of the island is Perry's Victory and International Peace Memorial, built to honor those who fought in the war of 1812. Golf carts, available for rent at the ferry landing, are a popular means of visitor transportation on the island. For Lake Erie island tourist infor-mation, visit shoresandislands.com. Anglers migrate to Lake Erie's waters during the spring and late summer to haul in stringers of walleye and yellow perch. Fishing charters by the hun-dreds are busy annually, helping anglers find fish for table fare and family photos.

Although Lake Erie is the shallowest of the five Great Lakes, its beauty runs deep, and there is no better observation point than atop a stone cliff at South Bass Island campground. After registering at the campground office, views of the lake will capture your attention. Because the campground is located on the windward side of South Bass Island, the waves are taller and the lake breeze is refreshing. After you force yourself to get back in your vehicle

Camping and water sports go hand in hand at South Bass Island State Park.

KEY INFORMATION

LOCATION: 1523 Catawba Avenue Put-In-Bay, Ohio 43456

CONTACT: 419-285-2112 (seasonal park office), 419-734-4424 (East Harbor State Park takes calls in off-season); parks.ohiodnr.gov/southbassisland

OPEN: April–mid-October; sites are walk-in only during April

SITES: 128, 58 tent-only

EACH SITE HAS: Picnic table, fire ring

WHEELCHAIR ACCESS: No specific ADA-accessible sites

ASSIGNMENT: Walk-in sites first come, first served; others may be reserved at 866-644-6727 or ohiostateparks.reserveamerica.com

REGISTRATION: At campground office; self-register at office if closed

AMENITIES: Showers, flush toilets, camp store, game room, boat ramp, fish-cleaning station, swimming beach, fishing pier

PARKING: At each site

FEE: $30

ELEVATION: 590 feet

RESTRICTIONS

PETS: On leash only in designated sites

QUIET HOURS: 10 p.m.–8 a.m.

FIRES: In fire ring, which must not be moved

ALCOHOL: Prohibited in public areas in every state park but may be consumed within the confines of a rented cabin, cabin site, lodge room, or campsite

VEHICLES: 1/site

OTHER: No mopeds or golf carts permitted in campground; gathering firewood prohibited; maximum 6 people/site

and head up into the shaded campground, sites 130–135 are on the left, at the edge of the stone cliff that gradually gains elevation. These six tent-only sites overlook a stony beach to the south and a busy boat ramp and concessions that rent jet skis in summer. They are well spaced, but be aware that they sit on a slope toward the cliff edge that has no safety fence.

The campground's paved lane splits after site 130, but you must go right as it is a one-way route. The narrow lane ramps up to a flat hilltop covered with a tight tree canopy created by a mix of mature hardwoods. Sites 1–70 cover the hilltop, sitting close together with only a few feet between them. This is where the RVs gather, and the view of Lake Erie is blocked by treetops growing along the cliff section. The sites featuring great lake views and breezes are reserved for tent campers only. After passing site 14 on the left, go straight to a T in the road and turn left. Site 75 is on the right and offers a tent spot up on a hump in the woods just a few steps from the parking pad. Sites 76 and 77 and sites 87–94 are the same. Across from site 87 are sites 78–86, sitting around the outside of a loop that drops down, away from the main campground lane. Those are tent-only sites as well.

Sites 95–101 are at the highest point on the lake cliff, and parking for those sites is in a shared lot on the right side of the lane as it turns downhill toward the campground entrance. Site 101 is the northernmost site and the most private. Each site is allowed 10 square yards of space. The lane continues south to the remaining lakeview sites. Sites 102–109 are set closer to the lane than the cliff edge but still provide amazing views of the lake. The next small parking area on the right is for sites 112–117, which are shoved out toward the edge of the rock face. A shower house is centrally located among the cliff-dwelling sites next to this parking area. If small children are part of your Lake Erie island campout, consider tent-only sites 106, 110, 111, 118, or 120, as they still provide decent views of the sunset but are staked out on the opposite side of the lane, a safe distance from the cliff. About 30 yards before you return to the one-way split, a fish-cleaning shed is available near tent-only site 122. Tent-only site 125 sits on a knoll, a grandstand of a site for the amazing Lake Erie show.

South Bass Island State Park

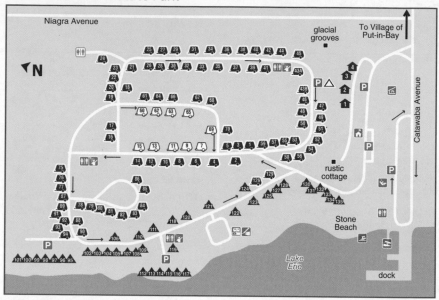

GETTING THERE

From the most northern point on Catawba Island, take the ferry (800-500-2421, miller ferry.com) north 3 miles to South Bass Island. Follow Langram Road northeast 0.8 mile to Meechen Road and turn left. Travel 0.4 mile northwest to Catawba Avenue, turn left, and the park entrance will be down the hill on the right.

GPS COORDINATES: N41° 38.518' W82° 50.154'

APPENDIX A

CAMPING EQUIPMENT CHECKLIST

COOKING UTENSILS
Aluminum foil
Bottles of salt, pepper, spices, sugar, cooking oil, and condiments in waterproof, spillproof containers
Bowls
Can opener
Cooking pots with lids
Cooler
Corkscrew
Cups (plastic or tin)
Dish soap (biodegradable), dishcloth, and towel
Dutch oven and fire pan
Fire starter
Flatware
Food of your choice
Frying pan and spatula
Lighter, matches in waterproof container
Paper towels
Plates
Pocketknife
Stove and fuel
Strainer
Tablecloth
Trash bags
Wooden spoon

SLEEPING GEAR
Pillow
Sleeping bag
Sleeping pad (inflatable or insulated)
Tent with ground tarp and rainfly

MISCELLANEOUS
Bath soap (biodegradable), washcloth, and towel
Camp chairs
Candles
Compass
Day pack
Extra batteries (for flashlight and electronics)
First aid kit (see page 5)
Flashlight/headlamp
GPS unit
Lantern
Maps (road, trail, topographic, etc.)
Moist towelettes
Saw/ax
Sunglasses
Toilet paper
Water bottle(s)
Wool blanket
Zip-top plastic bags

OPTIONAL
Barbecue grill
Binoculars
Books
Camera
Cards and board games
Field guides on bird, plant, and wildlife identification
Fishing rod and tackle

APPENDIX B

SOURCES OF INFORMATION

Ohio Department of Natural Resources (ODNR)

Division of Forestry
2045 Morse Road, Building H-1
Columbus, OH 43229-6693
877-247-8733
forestry.ohiodnr.gov

Division of Natural Areas and Preserves
2045 Morse Road, Building A-2
Columbus, OH 43229-6693
614-265-6453
naturepreserves.ohiodnr.gov

Division of Parks and Watercraft
2045 Morse Road, Building C-4
Columbus, OH 43229
614-265-6561; parks.ohiodnr.gov

Division of Wildlife
2045 Morse Road, Building G
Columbus, OH 43229-6693
800-WILDLIFE
wildlife.ohiodnr.gov

TourismOhio
P.O. Box 1001
Columbus, OH 43216-1001
800-BUCKEYE; ohio.org

U.S. Army Corps of Engineers
36007 OH 715
Warsaw, OH 43844-9534
740-824-4343; corpslakes.us

Wayne National Forest
13700 US 33
Nelsonville, OH 45764
740-753-0101; fs.usda.gov/wayne

American Electric Power
1 Riverside Plaza
Columbus, OH 43215-2372
614-716-1000
aep.com/recreation/areas/recreationland

Five Rivers MetroParks
409 E. Monument Ave., Third Floor
Dayton, OH 45402
937-275-7275; metroparks.org

Fredericktown Recreation District
P.O. Box 86
Fredericktown, Ohio 43019
740-694-8366; knoxchamber.com

Geauga Park District
9160 Robinson Road
Chardon, OH 44024
800-286-9516; geaugaparkdistrict.org

Hamilton County Park District
10245 Winton Road
Cincinnati, OH 45231
513-521-7275; greatparks.org

Muskingum Watershed Conservancy District
1319 Third St. NW
New Philadelphia, OH 44663
877-363-8500; mwcd.org

Sandusky County Park District
1970 Countryside Place
Fremont, OH 43420
419-334-4495; lovemyparks.com

Summit Metro Parks
975 Treaty Line Road
Akron, Ohio 44313
330-867-5511; summitmetroparks.org

INDEX

ABOUT THE AUTHOR

Robert Loewendick is an award-winning free-lance outdoors/travel writer and guidebook author, with work regularly published in print and on the internet. Although his passion for the outdoors lures him throughout the United States, Robert was born and raised in Ohio and still calls the Buckeye State his base camp. Whether fly-fishing a mountain stream, cruising a Great Lake for angling adventures, hiking miles of trails, or paddling across a placid lake, Robert's days outdoors regularly end at a campsite.

As a young boy, he explored the creeks, hills, and ravines of rural southeast Ohio daily. Roaming a neighboring ridgetop with a canvas backpack purchased at an Army surplus store, loaded with a canteen of water, a peanut butter and jelly sandwich, and a self-drawn map, fueled his fire for exploration early. Today, Robert shares his outdoors adventures with the goal of encouraging others to get outside more and connect with the real world. He believes that if one person, especially a child, is encouraged to explore outside more because of one of his productions, his work will have been successful.

Robert is an active member and past president of the professional outdoors journalism organization Outdoor Writers of Ohio.

DEAR CUSTOMERS AND FRIENDS,

SUPPORTING YOUR INTEREST IN OUTDOOR ADVENTURE, travel, and an active lifestyle is central to our operations, from the authors we choose to the locations we detail to the way we design our books. Menasha Ridge Press was incorporated in 1982 by a group of veteran outdoorsmen and professional outfitters. For many years now, we've specialized in creating books that benefit the outdoors enthusiast.

Almost immediately, Menasha Ridge Press earned a reputation for revolutionizing outdoors- and travel-guidebook publishing. For such activities as canoeing, kayaking, hiking, backpacking, and mountain biking, we established new standards of quality that transformed the whole genre, resulting in outdoor-recreation guides of great sophistication and solid content. Menasha Ridge Press continues to be outdoor publishing's greatest innovator.

The folks at Menasha Ridge Press are as at home on a whitewater river or mountain trail as they are editing a manuscript. The books we build for you are the best they can be, because we're responding to your needs. Plus, we use and depend on them ourselves.

We look forward to seeing you on the river or the trail. If you'd like to contact us directly, visit us at menasharidge.com. We thank you for your interest in our books and the natural world around us all.

SAFE TRAVELS,

Bob Sehlinger

BOB SEHLINGER
PUBLISHER